THE POWER

THAT PREVAILS

by

Rev. J. C. McPheeters, D. D.

First Fruits Press
Wilmore, Kentucky
c2012

asburyseminary.edu
800.2ASBURY
204 North Lexington Avenue
Wilmore, Kentucky 40390

First Fruits
THE ACADEMIC OPEN PRESS OF ASBURY SEMINARY

ISBN: 9780914368960

The Power that Prevails, by J.C. McPheeters.
First Fruits Press, © 2012
Pentecostal Publishing Company, © 1938

Digital version at
http://place.asburyseminary.edu/firstfruitsheritagematerial/11/

For all other uses, contact:

First Fruits Press
B.L. Fisher Library
Asbury Theological Seminary
204 N. Lexington Ave.
Wilmore, KY 40390
http://place.asburyseminary.edu/firstfruits

McPheeters, J. C. (Julian Claudius), 1889-1983.
    The power that prevails / by J.C. McPheeters.
    Wilmore, Ky. : First Fruits Press, c2012.
    Reprint. Previously published: Louisville, Ky. : Pentecostal Publishing
    Company, c1938.
    163 p. ; 21 cm
    ISBN: 9780914368960 (pbk.)
    1. Holiness. 2. Holy Spirit. I. Title
    BT767 .M297 2012

Cover design by Haley Hill

asburyseminary.edu
800.2ASBURY
204 North Lexington Avenue
Wilmore, Kentucky 40390

First Fruits
THE ACADEMIC OPEN PRESS OF ASBURY SEMINARY

THE POWER
THAT PREVAILS

BY

Rev. J. C. McPheeters, D. D.

Author of
"Sons of God," "Sunshine and Victory," "The Life Story of Lizzie H.
Glide," "Today With God," "Religious Trends of Today."

PENTECOSTAL PUBLISHING COMPANY
Louisville, Kentucky

INTRODUCTION

It is with real pleasure that I commend this volume, "The Power That Prevails," by Rev. J. C. McPheeters, D. D., Pastor of Glide Memorial Methodist Church, San Francisco, Calif., to the reading public, and especially to those who recognize the leadership of the Holy Spirit in true evangelism, the salvation of sinners and the sanctification of believers.

The Scriptures have spoken very plainly on the importance, in fact, the absolute necessity, of holiness, that we may enter into eternal rest at the conclusion of our life in the body in this world. The Scriptures not only proclaim the divine requirement of a full deliverance from sin, but they make abundant provision in Jesus Christ for our full salvation. and declare that, "He is able to do exceeding abundantly above all that we can ask or think." This is a wonderful promise and, no doubt true, that we never have nor ever shall be able to grasp the power of our Lord Jesus to deliver from sin, and to keep those who commit themselves to Him. Nothing can be more important than a Church in the world which is a real Bride of Christ, separate from sin, cleansed by the blood of our gracious Redeemer and filled with the Holy Spirit.

Dr. McPheeters has rendered a splendid service in writing this book on so vital and important a subject. We trust it may have a wide reading, and feel sure that it shall prove beneficial to those who thoughtfully and prayerfully peruse its pages.

Faithfully yours,

H. C. MORRISON.

CONTENTS

CHAPTER I

THE UPPER ROOM

The golden text of the Bible for the unsaved is the best known verse in the Bible: "For God so loved the world, that he gave his only begotten Son that whosoever believeth in him should not perish, but have everlasting life." (John 3:16). The golden text of the Bible for those who are saved is like unto it: "Christ also loved the church, and gave himself for it; that he might sanctify and cleanse it with the washing of water by the word, that he might present it to himself a glorious church, not having spot, or wrinkle, or any such thing; but that it should be holy and without blemish." (Eph. 5:25-27). These Scriptures seem to teach conclusively that the atoning sacrifice of Jesus on the cross included salvation for the sinner and holiness for the believer.

Most Christians agree that holiness is the supreme need of the church. There is, however, considerable disagreement as to the meaning of holiness. Some people approach this subject with a series of definitions. Definitions of terms have their place in the discussion of any subject, and we cannot go far in a discussion without coming, of necessity, to some definitions. But due to the large disagreement of terms and definitions concerning holiness we believe that it may perhaps be more profitable to make the approach by way of experience, and let the definitions come afterward. It may be well for us to say in the beginning that we believe in the Wesleyan doctrine of sanctification as taught by John Wesley and the early Methodists. The Bible is not lacking in clear and indisputable examples of saved people who later came into an experience through an epochal crisis which wielded a far-reaching influence upon their lives for both time and eternity.

The first of these examples which naturally comes to our attention is the case of the disciples of Jesus during His earthly ministry. There can be no doubt about these disciples being saved people. On one occasion Jesus told them: "Rejoice because your names are written in heaven." These plain words from the Master can leave no shadow of doubt as to these disciples being saved.

It was to these saved disciples that Jesus gave the command to tarry for the coming of the Holy Ghost. Luke speaks of this farewell command of Jesus to His disciples in these words: "And, being assembled together with them, commanded them that they should not depart from Jerusalem, but wait for the promise of the Father, which, saith he, ye have heard of me. For John truly baptized with water; but ye shall be baptized with the Holy Ghost not many days hence." (Acts 1:4, 5). In connection with the command this promise is also given: "But ye shall receive power, after the Holy Ghost is come upon you: and ye shall be witnesses unto me both in Jerusalem and in Judea, and in Samaria, and unto the uttermost part of the earth." (Acts 1:8).

The record is very clear that these disciples of Jesus, in obedience to the command, obtained the fulfillment of the promise. No more thrilling story is to be found on all the pages of literature than the account of that experience which came to the disciples at the close of that memorable ten-day prayer meeting in the Upper Room. Something happened to the hundred and twenty in that Upper Room which was tremendous in results, both in their individual lives and in the life of the world. That historic prayer meeting has shed the glow of its precious light across the pathway of more than nineteen centuries.

At Pentecost cowardice was turned into holy boldness, timidity and fear into strength and courage, doubt and vacillation into stalwart faith and a gibraltar of solidity. These disciples, although few in number, and without prestige or worldly standing, made such an impact upon Jerusalem as the city had never known. The glory and the rapture in their hearts could not be restrained. The fires that burned within leaped with more avidity than any prairie fire that ever raced across the long stretches of the western plains. No Upper Room could contain them. They must hit the dusty trails of human need. From that Upper Room they rushed to the streets of the city with a glorious proclamation. Multitudes rushed to hear them from every quarter of the city as they stood upon the streets and proclaimed the glories of their newfound experience.

It was evident to all the world that something had happened to these one hundred and twenty humble followers of Jesus. They were not the same disciples who had entered the Upper Room ten days previous. The animation in their voices, the radiance of their faces, the boldness and authority of the words were unmistakable evidence that something of a tremendous nature had taken place. Cold arguments and bold opposition broke down under the pressure of the floodtide of this rushing Pentecostal stream of dynamic experience which broke forth with irresistible pressure from the Rock of Ages.

The great Pentecostal revival moved through the city of Jerusalem with cyclonic effect. The tall sons of evil fell in its pathway by the thousands. Fairly breath-taking are the words which summarize the results: "And the same day there were added unto them about three thousand souls." The whole city was electrified with the pressure of the new found experience of the disciples. A stream of spiritual power was released in the world which no forces of Hell could check. All of this was a fulfillment of the words which Jesus had formerly spoken to His disciples: "In the last day, that great day of the feast, Jesus stood and cried, saying, If any man thirst, let him come unto me and drink. He that believeth on me, as the scripture hath said, out of his belly shall flow rivers of living water. But this spake he of the Spirit, which they that believe on him should receive: for the Holy Ghost was not yet given; because that Jesus was not yet glorified." (John 7:37-29).

A rushing mountain stream fed by perennial springs bursting forth from hill, crag and canyon, not only has in it power which may turn the wheels of industry and furnish the lights of a great city, but it also has in it a purifying and cleansing element of inestimable worth.

The Scripture seems to be clear in its teaching that the disciples not only received power at Pentecost, but also cleansing and purity. This fact is made plain in the words of Peter before the council at Jerusalem, when he said: "And God which knoweth the hearts, bear them witness, giving them the Holy Ghost, even as he did unto us; and put no difference between us and them, purifying their hearts by faith."

The genius of the first century church was the genius of the Pentecostal experience. Whenever there has been defeat or decadence of any nature in the church it has been due largely to a lack of this experience in cleansing and enduement. Some one has said: "Twentieth century

Christians have become *problem conscious;* while
the first century Christians were *power conscious."* The modern church has often become
more concerned about the Forum than the Upper Room; more eager for "up-to-dateishness"
than for holiness. We have become expert as
diagosticians, but weak as practitioners. We
have become more concerned about current
news from the tension spots of the world than
about the current news from heaven as the only
remedy for these tension spots. The result is
that wherever there is a reversal of this Pentecostal emphasis, problems are in the saddle riding the church, instead of the church being in
the sadde, riding and directing her problems,
with victory perched upon her banner, and a
triumphant glory radiating from her soul.

CHAPTER II

EMPHASIS OF THE FIRST CENTURY CHURCH

As we read the book of Acts we are greatly impressed with the emphasis which the apostles place upon the experience of holiness of heart and life for those already saved. We are also impressed with the fact that they urged saved believers to enter immediately into this experience, if they had not entered such a Canaan experience.

In the eighth chapter of Acts we have an account of the great revival in Samaria. The human leader in this revival was Philip. It was not an easy field, for the Jews and the Samaritans had no dealings with each other. During His earthly ministry Jesus had broken over this chasm of preudice, and surprised His disciples by engaging in conversation with the woman at the well. This woman accepted Christ, and turned many of her own city unto Him. In the conversion of the woman at the well, and the great revival under the preaching of Philip, we see the power of divine grace in overcoming seemingly insurmountable difficulties.

The dominant note in the preaching of Philip was the saving power of Jesus Christ. "Then Philip went down to the city of Samaria, and preached Christ, unto them." (Acts 8:5). Every great revival in the church has been characterized by this kind of preaching.

Book reviews, current events, moving pictures, human philosophy, nor modernism will never bring a revival. Jesus is the only remedy for the souls of men. He is the Great Physician. He has said: "If I be lifted up I will draw all men unto me." The spiritual dearth of this age is due to the lack of uplifting Jesus Christ as the all-sufficient and only Savior of mankind.

Spiritual depressions have always come to the church when she has been sidetracked to things other than the preaching of Christ. One of the alarming trends of the present day is the suspending of the Sunday evening service in churches all over the nation. Our darkened churches on Sunday evenings present a tragic testimony of spiritual decline in the land. The faithful presentation of an uplifted Christ in these vacant pulpits on Sunday evenings would turn the defeat expressed in the darkened church into triumph and victory.

One of the remarkable examples in modern times of the power of preaching Christ was the great revival in Chicago under the leadership of Dwight L. Moody during the World's Fair of 1893. When Moody arrived on the ground at the beginning of the campaign, he said: "We shall beat the World's Fair." The greatest day of the exposition was Chicago day, when the theaters did not even dare to open, believing that everybody would be at the fair. On that day

Mr. Moody hired Central Music Hall for a continuous meeting from 9 A. M. to 6 P. M. Although the hall was five miles down-town from the fair grounds, it was continuously jammed.

The great evangelistic campaign even "beat a circus!" When Forepaugh's Circus came to the city, announcement was made for two Sunday performances. The big tent seated ten thousand, with room for an additional ten thousand in the arena. Mr. Moody secured the tent for a Sunday morning service. The management laughed at such an attempt. The result was that the great tent was packed for the gospel service, and the crowd was so small for the circus in the afternoon that further Sunday performances were discontinued.

At the opening of the campaign, Mr. Moody said to his workers: "Let's not spend time splitting hairs in theology, and wrangling about creeds. Let's go to work and save lost souls. Our gospel is the only hope of the drunkard, the gambler, the harlot, the lost on the streets of Chicago. Oh, let us go and save them! I would rather save one soul from death than have a monument of gold reaching from my grave to the heavens!" The attendance during the campaign reached as high as 71,000 for a single day, and multiplied thousands accepted Christ.

Moody held his last conference with his workers at the close of the Fair on the night of October 31. He remained alone in his room, long after midnight, after his workers had departed. He fell on his knees and sobbed aloud a prayer: "Oh, my dear Lord, after these wonderful days I'm so grateful thou didst not let me disobey the heavenly vision! I thank thee for the shipwreck! The old gospel has lost nothing of its power! And it never will! Dear Lord, I can say tonight with Simeon, 'Now lettest thou thy servant depart in peace, for mine eyes have seen thy glory!' "

The great revival under Philip, with its counterparts in modern times, is described in these words: "For unclean spirits, crying with loud voice, came out of many that were possessed with them: and many taken with palsies, and that were lame, were healed. And there was great joy in that city." (Acts 8:7, 8). The joy which a great revival brings surpasses anything that the world has to offer. The joy of the world, as compared to the joy of the Lord, is as the starlight compared to the zenith of the noon-day sun.

Following the revival at Samaria, the apostles at Jerusalem sent two of their strongest numbers down to Samaria to lead the new converts into the great Pentecostal experience which they themselves had received in the Upper Room. "Now when the apostles which were at Jerusalem heard that Samaria had received the word of God, they sent unto them Peter and John: who, when they were come down, prayed

for them, that they might receive the Holy
Ghost: (For as yet he was fallen upon none of
them: only they were baptized in the name of
the Lord Jesus). Then laid they their hands on
them, and they received the Holy Ghost." (Acts
8:14-17).

The record here is very clear in setting forth
two great epochal experiences of far-reaching
consequence in the lives of the converts of the
Samaritan revival. There is no room left to
doubt the genuineness of the converts under the
preaching of Philip. Unclean spirits came out
of them, and they had great joy. These are certainly definite characteristics of new converts.
It is very evident that the apostles at Jerusalem
recognized the great importance of leading these
new converts into the Upper Room experience
which had come to them at Pentecost.

Is not such a need still apparent in the
church? Do we not find multitudes in the church
who fall into the same category, in the matter of
experience, of the apostles before Pentecost? Is
it not a fact that we have a great many whose
salvation we could not doubt for one moment,
who are powerless and whose lives are bearing
very little fruit for Christ? Surely there is a
remedy for this barrenness and deficiency. God
is able. Yes, He "is able to do exceeding abundantly above all that we ask or think, according
to the power that worketh in us.' (Eph. 3:20).

The first century church placed large empha-

sis upon the importance of bringing the new
converts into the Pentecostal experience. Has
the modern church gained anything when she
has dropped this emphasis from her teaching
and preaching? Has neglect in this matter sent
out more missionaries, raised more money, and
brought down more revivals on the people? Has
it made the church more joyous, and increased
her stride? Has it contributed to filling up the
vacant pews, raising the church debt, and re-
plenishing the church treasury? The plain facts
are before us. Put the church on the witness
stand and let her answer these questions in the
light of the day of judgment. What will her
answer be?

Yea, but some are ready to say, even in the
face of the lack of purity and enduement in the
modern church: "We no longer need the old-
fashioned doctrine of the first century Christians concerning the Baptism with the Holy
Ghost, and of the early Methodists concerning
Perfect Love. We live in a new day and a new
age, and we must now make a new approach."
Since when did carnality in human nature become so refined and changed under the influence
of modern culture that it demands a "new approach?" Again, the facts of history are to the
contrary as to any change in carnality in human
nature. When such a change comes in carnality,
then it will be time to advocate our boasted "new
approach." But until such change actually

comes in carnlaity, we should proclaim no less a gospel than was proclaimed by John, the beloved, "The blood of Jesus Christ his Son cleanseth from all sin," and also by Jesus himself, "But ye shall receive power, after the Holy Ghost is come upon you."

CHAPTER III

FULL SALVATION

As we read the book of Acts we are greatly impressed with the emphasis which the Early Church placed upon the experience which the hundred and twenty disciples received in the Upper Room. The record is clear that this experience was not limited to those who received the great Pentecostal baptism on the day of Pentecost. The leaders of the church of the first century regarded it of primal importance to bring the new converts into that blessed experience of cleansing and enduement which they themselves received on the day of Pentecost.

We have discussed the great revival in the city of Samaria under the preaching of Philip, when many were converted, bringing great joy to the city. The leaders of the church at Jerusalem sent Peter and John to the scene of the revival following the preaching of Philip, who led the new converts into the Pentecostal experience which had come to the hundred and twenty in the Upper Room.

Another remarkable example portraying the emphasis which God placed upon the Pentecostal baptism in the early church is found in the tenth chapter of the book of Acts. This chapter gives us the story of Cornelius, the Roman Centurion, and his baptism with the Holy Ghost under the preaching of Peter.

Cornelius, like the disciples before Pentecost, and, like the Samaritan converts before they heard the preaching of Peter and John, was undoubtedly a saved man. The statements of the Scriptures are clear and plain as to his relationship with God. He is described as "a devout man," "one that feared God," "gave much alms to the people," "prayed to God always." We have a further statement that his prayers and gifts were accepted by the Lord: "Thy prayers and thy alms are come up for a memorial before God." Cornelius further quotes the words of the heavenly messenger who stood by him thus: "Cornelius, thy prayer is heard, and thine alms are had in remembrance in the sight of God."

There is no promise in the Bible that the prayer of the wicked is heard for anything other than for his salvation. The wicked are encouraged to pray for salvation in the promise, "Whosoever shall call upon the name of the Lord shall be saved." Otherwise the prayer of the wicked is unacceptable to the Lord, as expressed in the words: "The sacrifice of the wicked is an abomination to the Lord: but the prayer of the upright is his delight." (Prov. 15:8). Again we are told by the Psalmist: "If I regard iniquity in my heart the Lord will not hear me: but verily God hath heard me; he hath attended to the voice of my prayer." (Ps. 66:18, 19). Answered prayer is presented by the Psalmist as an evidence that iniquity has been taken from his heart.

There is no promise in the Bible that God accepts the alms of those who are not in a saved relationship with the Lord. The teaching on this subject in the Old Testament seems well summarized in the words of Malachi, when he spoke concerning the gifts of the wicked in these words: "I have no pleasure in thee, saith the Lord of hosts, neither will I accept an offering at your hand." (Mal. 1:10). The New Testament teaching of the acceptability of the gifts of the sinner is summarized in the words of the Apostle Paul: "And though I bestow all my goods to feed the poor, and though I give my body to be burned, and have not love, it profiteth me nothing." (1 Cor. 13:3).

The fact that both the prayers and the alms of Cornelius were accepted by the Lord indicate that he was a saved man. There is a Scripture statement which might seem to the contrary which should command our attention in this connection. Peter, in the course of his address before the council at Jerusalem, gives a description of the vision, as related by Cornelius: "And he showed us how he had seen an angel in his house which stood and said unto him, Send men to Joppa, and call for Simon, who shall tell thee words whereby thou and all thy house shall be saved." Some theologians cite this Scripture as evidence that Cornelius was an unsaved man previous to the visit of Peter.

This Scripture must be considered in the light of all of the statements concerning Cornelius. When considered in the light of the statements which seem to indicate clearly that Cornelius was a saved man, the statement made by Peter before the council at Jerusalem does not seem to indicate primary salvation. Justification is primary salvation, and it was only this primary salvation which Cornelius enjoyed. Sanctification is full salvation, and glorification is final salvation. It was salvation in the fuller sense which Cornelius needed. This is undoubtedly the need of multitudes in the church today. Salvation in this fuller sense brings the same note of triumph and victory that characterized the church of the first century.

In the introduction of his sermon in the home of Cornelius, Peter stated that Cornelius was accepted of the Lord: "Of a truth I perceive that God is no respecter of persons: but in every nation he that feareth him and worketh righteousness is accepted with him." Peter's statement seems conclusive that Cornelius was accepted of the Lord. Peter further states: "The word which God sent unto the children of Israel, preaching peace by Jesus Christ: (he is Lord of all:) that word, I say, you know which was published throughout all Judea, and began from Galilee after the baptism which John preached." This statement of Peter reveals the fact that Cornelius had come in contact with the great

Pentecostal revival which had spread throughout Judea, "preaching peace by Jesus Christ."
Peter, in describing the contact which Cornelius
had already had with this revival, says: "This
word, I say, ye know, which was published
throughout all Judea."

It had been some eight or ten years since
the Pentecostal revival had begun to spread
throughout Judea. Cornelius had evidently come
under its influence to the extent that he had entered into a state of primary salvation. It is
true that he had not been baptized, but it is not
uncommon to find people who come under the
influence of a great revival and enter a state of
salvation without receiving immediately water
baptism.

The result of the preaching of Peter to Cornelius and his household brought the same Pentecostal baptism which came to the hundred and
twenty in the Upper Room. "While Peter yet
spake these words the Holy Ghost fell on all of
them which heard the word." In his address
before the council at Jerusalem, Peter states
that the experience which came to Cornelius on
this occasion was the same as that which came
to the disciples in the Upper Room: "For as
much then as God gave them the like gift as he
did unto us, who believed on the Lord Jesus
Christ: what was I that I could withstand God?"

Cornelius stands as a type of many saved
people in our churches today who stand in need

of the Upper Room experience.   If we can bring
the church back to Pentecost we will again see a
new daring, zeal, purity of life and holy unction
which will make a mighty impact upon the
world.   Victory will be perched upon our ban-
ners, where now we are trailing in defeat.   We
will turn back the onrushing tides of sin and
iniquity now deluging the world everywhere,
and will cause the world to again speak of the
church: "These that have turned the world upside down are come hither also."

CHAPTER IV

THE WAY OF GOD MORE PERFECT

The book of Acts gives us a number of instances of saved people not yet having received the Baptism with the Holy Spirit. Three cases have already been discussed: the disciples before Pentecost, the Samaritan converts previous to the preaching of Peter and John, and Cornelius previous to the visit of Peter. Expositors of various schools of interpretation stand fairly well agreed that in the first two instances we have examples of people who were saved, having their names written in heaven prior to receiving the Baptism with the Holy Ghost. While their theological implications vary, the unity of the verdict relative to having examples of people saved previous to receiving the Baptism with the Holy Ghost is significant. The case of Cornelius is more of a debated question among expositors; the evidence, however, seems conclusive to the writer that Cornelius was in a saved relationship with God prior to the visit of Peter, when he received the Baptism with the Holy Spirit.

The Christians of the church of the first century were dominated by a holy passion to lead all believers into that definite epochal Pentecostal Baptism which came to the one hundred and twenty in the Upper Room. This was a matter of primary importance with them. It occupied a place of first consideration in their program. We are forcibly impressed with this fact as we read the book of Acts.

Another example of this primary emphasis is found in the nineteenth chapter of Acts. Paul found certain disciples at Ephesus, and his first question to these disciples was, "Have ye received the Holy Ghost since ye believed?" Do we find here another example of saved people who have not received the Baptism with the Holy Ghost? There is evidence that these disciples had come to repentance and the forgiveness of their sins under the eloquent preaching of Apollos. The preaching of Apollos is described in these words: "This man was instructed in the way of the Lord; and being fervent in the spirit, he spake and taught diligently the things of the Lord, knowing only the baptism of John." (Acts 18:25). The baptism of John was unto repentance. John was careful to tell those who repented and were baptized under his preaching, of the Christ, and of His baptism with the Holy Ghost. He made it clear to his converts that he himself was only the forerunner of one whose shoes he was not worthy to unloose.

Apollos is described as a man "instructed in the way of the Lord." He was instructed in matters pertaining to primary salvation, but he himself needed instruction in the deeper way of holiness, as is indicated by his experience with Aquila and Priscilla, who "expounded unto him the way of God more perfectly." (Acts 18:26). Apollos was "fervent in spirit," and "he spake and taught diligently the things of the Lord." These are commendable qualities, and are very essential elements for the preacher of the gospel. But as to the deeper aspects of the Christian experience, he himself was lacking. This being true, he did not lead his converts beyond the level of his own experience. It is a well-known fact that, as a rule, people do not rise in their religious experience above the standards of their ministers.

These disciples which Paul found at Ephesus evidently measured up to the standards which they had received under the preaching of Apollos. Paul speaks of them as disciples and believers. The word "disciple" after the death and resurrection of Jesus, came to mean a follower of Christ. "And the disciples were called Christians first at Antioch." (Acts 11:26). The word "believer" was also used in reference to those who had become followers of Christ. "And believers were the more added to the Lord, multitudes both of men and women." (Acts 5:14). Paul exhorted Timothy: "But be thou an example of the believers." (1 Tim. 4:12). Since these disciples had been under the preaching of

Apollos it is quite reasonable to suppose that they partook of some of his Christian qualities, such as "being fervent in spirit," and teaching "diligently the things of the Lord."

It is quite evident that Paul was speaking to saved believers when he inquired of them, "Have ye received the Holy Ghost since ye believed?" The variations found in different translations of this passage have given ground for discussion. The rendering of the American Revised Version is, "Did ye receive the Holy Spirit when ye believed?" The translations of Moffatt and Goodspeed are, in substance, the same as the American Revised Version. Dr. W. B. Godbey gives the following translation of the entire verse: "Did ye receive the Holy Ghost, having believed? And they said, But we did not hear that the Holy Ghost is given." The literal Interlinear Translation from the Greek more nearly coincides with the rendering of Dr. Godbey, than either the rendering of the American or Revised Version, Moffatt, or Goodspeed. The Interlinear Translation is as follows: ("The) Spirit Holy did ye receive, having believed? And they said to him, Not even if (the) Spirit Holy is, did we hear." The literal rendering seems to clearly indicate that the Baptism with the Holy Ghost is an experience for those who have already believed, that is, those who have accepted Christ as their personal Savior. Some people use the Revised Version as evidence that the Baptism with the Holy

Ghost comes at the time of regeneration and is not necessarily a distinct work of grace coming subsequent. The Interlinear Translation, however, seems to clearly indicate that the Baptism with the Holy Ghost comes after believing and accepting Christ as Savior.

Those who press the rendering of the American Revised Version in support of the position that the Baptism with the Holy Ghost comes at the time of regeneration, should consider well some of the facts which are involved in accepting the American Revised rendering. The facts briefly, are these: (1) First, we have believers who did not receive the Baptism of the Holy Ghost at the time they believed. (2). They were urged to immediately seek and obtain this Baptism. (3) The conditions which prevailed among these disciples at Ephesus in having believed without receiving the Baptism of the Holy Ghost, is also the state of a large percent of the Christian believers in the church of the present day. (4) Christian believers of the present day who have not received the Baptism with the Holy Ghost should be urged to seek and obtain this baptism immediately, just as Paul urged the disciples at Ephesus.

Only recently, I was engaged in conversation on the subject of holiness with one of the representative pastors of Methodism in the leading church of his denomination in a city of seventy-five thousand people. He brought up the subject himself, seeming eager for a frank, brotherly discussion of this important matter. He has never accepted the theology of holiness as involving an epochal experience of cleansing and enduement subsequent to regeneration. But in the course of the discussion he was frank to say: "I realize that I have a very wonderful people in my congregation. Many of them are tithers, and they manifest an unusual degree of loyalty to the church. However, I realize they are lacking in power. Unless something comes about in Methodism to bring this enduement which I realize is so greatly needed in my own congregation, we are undone as a people."

Such a testimony as this could be multiplied today, by many prominent pastors in Methodism. Something is lacking; something is badly needed. The Apostle Paul gave the key to that something, and that which is lacking, in his frank and open question to the disciples at Ephesus: "Have ye received the Holy Ghost since ye believed?" One thing is certain: Methodism has found no message to improve on that preached by John Wesley and the early fathers concerning the doctrine of holiness as a definite experience for believers to receive, live, witness to, and triumph in, both in life and in death, and throughout eternity.

CHAPTER V.

The subject of holiness occupies a major place in the epistles of the New Testament. The writer of the epistle to the Hebrews says: "Follow peace with all men, and holiness, without which no man shall see the Lord.' (Heb. 12:14). Holiness was provided in the atonement which Christ made upon the cross. This fact is clearly revealed in a number of very plain statements of the Scripture. "By the which will we are sanctified through the offering of the body of Jesus Christ once for all." (Heb. 10:10). "For by one offering he hath perfected for ever them that are sanctified." (Heb. 10:14). "Wherefore Jesus also, that he might sanctify the people with his own blood, suffered without the gate." (Heb. 13:12). "The blood of Jesus Christ his Son cleanseth us from all sin." (1 John 1:7).

Paul prays for the sanctification of the Thessalonian church in these words: "And the very God of peace sanctify you wholly; and I pray God your whole spirit and soul and body be preserved blameless unto the coming of our Lord Jesus Christ." (1 Thess. 5:23).

Whatever the grounds for debate upon particular views or interpretations of holiness, there can be no grounds for debate upon the fact that the New Testament places a major emphasis upon holiness. Is this emphasis still maintained in the average modern church? I fear the verdict stands against us. We have often been more concerned about raising quotas than we have about bringing people into holiness. The sad retrenchment in the missionary program of the major denominations, within recent years, indicates that we have not even been greatly concerned about the quotas. Is it not possible that there may be a very vital connection between our lack of emphasis upon holiness and the retrenchment in our missionary programs? Can we recover the lost ground of recent years without returning to the same New Testament emphasis? An official of one of the great denominational missionary boards of the country recently said to me: "It no longer impresses our people to tell them how much they are spending for chewing gum, cosmetics, jewelry or tobacco, as compared to what they are spending for the evangelization of the world. The quoting of statistics concerning the great need and the small supply to meet this need is failing to find a proper response in the hearts of our people. Some deeper strata and firmer foundation on which to build our missionary program must be found, or we are doomed to continued retrenchment."

The modern church has been so much concerned about the branches of the tree that she has neglected the roots. The branches have been withered, as is indicated by the vast retrenchments in missionary programs, the closing of churches on Sunday nights, and the decrease in church and Sunday school attendance in wide areas of the church. Can we hope for recovery by temporarily freshening up the branches? I hardly think so. There is danger that in our efforts to restore the life of the tree that we depend upon attractive substitutes for the one thing needful: holiness.

Paul was a great strategist. He dealt with problems at their source. He sought treatment for the disease instead of the symptoms. When he found certain disciples at Ephesus, he well knew that those disciples were the key for reaching that great city. He also knew that they would not be equivalent to the task without the Baptism with the Holy Ghost. His first message to these disciples was concerning this Baptism. Their ready response to his message resulted in these few disciples receiving the Pentecostal Baptism, and becoming numbered among those who "turn the world upside down."

Paul's first epistle to the Thessalonians furnishes us another remarkable example of his deep concern about leading the church into the experience of holiness. Paul founded the church at Thessalonica following his exit from Philippi, after being cast into the Philippian jail. The great revival at Thessalonica, under the preaching of Paul and his helpers, was intercepted by persecutors, who made it necessary for a retreat from the city. Paul continued his missionary itinerary to Berea, Athens and Corinth. It was at Corinth he sojourned for eighteen months, and from whence he wrote both epistles to the Thessalonians.

The standing of believers in the church of Christ is well portrayed in the first chapter of the first epistle. The salutation describes them as being "in God the Father and in the Lord Jesus Christ." Their standing with the Lord was such that Paul gave thanks to God for them: "We give thanks to God always for you all, making mention of you in our prayers." This church was characterized by a "work of faith, and labor of love, and patience of hope in our Lord Jesus Christ, in the sight of God and our Father." They are also spoken of as the elect of God: "Knowing, brethren beloved, your election of God."

Paul did the preaching under which the Thessalonians were converted, and there can be no doubt but that a genuine work of grace prevailed under his ministry. The gospel came to them "in much assurance." "For our gospel came not unto you in word only, but also in power, and in the Holy Ghost, and in much assurance." Their loyalty to the word of God and their joy in the Holy Ghost is described: "And ye became followers of us, and of the Lord, having received the word in much affliction, with joy of the Holy Ghost." They are described as good examples: "So that ye were ensamples to all that believe in Macedonia and Achaia." These Thessalonian Christians were also characterized by a great missionary zeal: "For from you sounded out the word of the Lord not only in Macedonia and Achaia, but also in every place your faith to God-ward is spread abroad." They had turned from their worldly idols to serve the Lord: "Ye turned from God to serve the living and true God." They were living in expectancy of the return of the Lord. "And to wait for his Son from heaven, whom he raised from the dead, even Jesus, which delivered us from the wrath to come."

The description given in the first chapter of First Thessalonians portrays to us a remarkable people. Comparatively few churches of the present day measure up to the standards to which this church had attained.

The third chapter of the epistle reveals that this church was not a backslidden church. Paul became so concerned about them that he sent Timothy to inquire concerning their spiritual progress: "For this cause, when I could no longer forbear, I sent to know your faith, lest by some means the tempter had tempted you, and our labor be in vain." (1 Thess. 3:5). When Timothy brought back a good report from the church Paul says: "Therefore, brethren, we were comforted over you in all our affliction and distress by your faith: for now we live, if ye stand fast in the Lord."

The third chapter of the epistle also reveals that this church, so remarkable in many respects, was lacking in something of very great importance. It was so eminently important that Paul was praying night and day about it. He says: "Night and day praying exceedingly that we might see your face, and might perfect that which is lacking in your faith." That which was lacking is described in the closing verse of the chapter: "To the end he may stablish your hearts unblameable in holiness before God, even our Father at the coming of our Lord Jesus Christ with all the saints."

In the fourth chapter we are told that God has made provision for the supply of this great need of the church to be established "unblameable in holiness before God." This provision is thus described: "For this is the will of God, even your sanctification." Sanctification is a fortification against backsliding, as indicated in the closing words of the same verse: "that ye should abstain from fornication." The provision for the great need of the church to be established in holiness is further indicated: "For God hath not called us unto uncleanness, but unto holiness."

In the closing words of the epistle we have this promise: "Faithful is he that calleth you, who also will do it." The apostle also warns of the danger in rejecting the provision which God has made: "He therefore that rejecteth, rejecteth not man, but God." The glorious heritage of the church is holiness, to be sought, obtained, and witnessed to in this life, through the merits of the blood of Christ, who, "that he might sanctify the people with his own blood, suffered without the gate."

CHAPTER VI

"A CLOUD OF WITNESSES"

One of the laws of pragmatic philosophy, so much relied upon in certain camps of modern thought, is: "Truth is tested by the practical consequences of belief." Under this law the doctrine of holiness meets the test of modern scholarship.

There is an array of evidence in personal experience and testimony to holiness coming as a definite epochal experience subsequent to regeneration, which no fair-minded thinker can dismiss with a sheer wave of the hand. John Wesley had more of the scientific attitude than some of the boasted liberals of the present day in matters pertaining to Christian experience. No man, since the days of the apostles, has made a more thoroughly scientific investigation of Christian experience than John Wesley. He sifted Christian experience and testimony with the utmost scrutiny in the light of the Word of God. The result of Mr. Wesley's searching investigation, extending over many years, is clearly revealed in his writings and his own personal testimony.

Mr. Wesley gave special attention to the investigation of the experience of holiness, both in the Word of God and in the lives of those who professed to have attained such an experience. The summary of his investigation in the Word of God is expressed in the conclusion of his "Plain Account of Christian Perfection": "It is the doctrine of St. Paul, St. James, St. Peter, and St. John, and no otherwise Mr. Wesley's than as it is of every one who preaches the pure and the whole gospel. I tell you as plain as I can speak, where and when I found this. I found it in the oracles of God, in the Old and New Testaments, when I read them with no other view than to save my own soul."

The thoroughness of Mr. Wesley's investigation of the experience of those who professed holiness or sanctification, is summarized in his own words: "We asked them the most seaching questions we could devise. They answered every one without hesitation and with the utmost simplicity, so that we were fully persuaded that they did not deceive themselves." He is also careful to state that he derived his information first hand, without relying on the testimony of others. In speaking of this fact, he says: "Not trusting to the testimony of others, I carefully examined most of these myself; and in London alone I found six hundred and fifty-two members of our Society who were exceeding clear in their experience, and whose testimony I could see no reason to doubt."

Both the Scriptures and the testimony of a multitude of believers professing the experience of sanctification, led Mr. Wesley to teach sanctification as an instantaneous work. In a letter to Messrs. Maxfield, Bell, and Owen, dated Nov. 1, 1776, he said: "You have over and over denied instantaneous sanctification, but I have known and taught it (and so has my brother, as our writings show) above these twenty years." In his sermon on "The Scripture Way of Salvation" he gives a personal testimony in these words: "I have continually testified, in private and in public, that we are sanctified, as well as justified by faith."

John Fletcher is well known as "Wesley's designated successor." Robert Southey of the Church of England said of Fletcher: "No church has ever possessed a more apostolic minister." Robert Hall, the distinguished Baptist minister, said: "Fletcher is a seraph who burns with the ardor of divine love." Dr. Dixon, a distinguished Methodist minister, summarized the character of Fletcher in a striking sentence: "I conceive Fletcher to have been the most holy man who has been upon the earth since the apostolic age."

John Fletcher possessed a fiery, passionate spirit which proved a source of no little trouble after his conversion. He spent many hours praying for victory over his own temper. In describing the experience which came to him in sanctification, Fletcher says: "Last Monday evening he (God) spoke to me by these words:

'Reckon yourself, therefore, to be dead indeed to sin, but alive unto God through Jesus Christ our Lord.' I obeyed the voice of God; I now obey it, and tell you all, to the praise of his love, I am free from sin, dead unto sin, and alive unto God . . . And I will declare unto you, in the presence of God the Holy Trinity, that I am now dead indeed unto sin and alive unto God, through Jesus Christ, who is my indwelling holiness, my all in all." Fletcher became one of the ablest defenders and exponents of the doctrine of entire sanctification among the early Methodists.

Bishop Richard Whatcoat, who was a colleague of Francis Asbury, had a clear and happy conversion, followed subsequently by a definite experience of sanctification. In speaking of his sanctification, after describing his conversion, Bishop Whatcoat says: "My faith and love grew stronger, but I soon found that, though I was justified freely, yet I was not wholly sanctified. This brought me into deep concern, and confirmed my resolution to admit of no peace or truce with the evils which I still found in my heart. . . . After many sharp and painful conflicts, and many gracious visitations also, on the 28th of March, 1761, my soul was drawn out and engaged in a manner it never was before. Suddenly I was stripped of all but love. And in this happy state, rejoicing evermore and in everything giving thanks, I continued for some years with little intermission or abatement, wanting

THE POWER THAT PREVAILS

nothing for soul or body more than I received
from day to day."

When Francis Asbury wrote the memoir of
his colleague, Bishop Whatcoat, to be read before the conferences, he closed with this interesting summary:

"Converted September 3, 1758.
Sanctified March 28, 1761.
Began to travel in 1769.
Elected Superintendent in May, 1800.
Died in Dover, Delaware, July 5, 1806."

Francis Asbury was well known for his
preaching on the subject of Perfect Love.   It
was one of his favorite themes.   In his diary he
records both the number of people who were
saved, and also the number of people who were
sanctified in some of his great camp meetings.

Bishop E. E. Hoss has given to the church a
splendid biography of William McKendree, the
first native American bishop of the Methodist
Episcopal Church.   In this biography we find a
description of the conversion of Bishop McKendree given in McKendree's own words: "My convictions were renewed; they were deep and
pungent.   The great deep of my heart was brok-
en up, its desperately wicked nature was dis-
closed, and the awfully ruinous consequences
clearly appeared.   My repentance was sincere.
I was desirous of salvation, and became willing
to be saved on any terms; and after a sore and

sorrowful travail of three days, which were employed in hearing Mr. Easter and in fasting and prayer, while that man of God was showing a large congregation the way of salvation by faith with a clearness which at the same time astonished and encouraged me, I ventured my all on Christ. In a moment my soul was delivered of a burden too heavy to be borne, and joy instantly succeeded sorrow. For a short space of time I was fixed in silent admiration, giving glory to God for his unspeakable goodness to such an unworthy creature."

Following this description of Bishop McKendree's conversion Bishop Hoss says: "The early Methodists were diligently taught to grow in grace, and to go on to perfection. Nothing less than this, they were assured, should be the goal of all of their striving."

Bishop Hoss describes McKendree's sanctification by again quoting McKendree's own words: "The more I sought the blessing of sanctification, the more I felt the need of it. In its pursuit my soul grew in grace and in the faith that overcomes the world. One morning I walked into the field, and while I was musing such an overwhelming power of the Divine Being overshadowed me as I had never experienced before. Unable to stand, I sank to the ground more than filled with transport. My cup ran over, and I shouted aloud."

In commenting on this experience of McKendree's sanctification, Bishop Hoss says: "Let whoever will undertake to explain an experience like that as something that began and ended in McKendree's own mind. I cannot be guilty of such irreverence; neither have I any desire to explain it in terms of technical theology. The only thing that a believer can say is that God was in it. It did not terminate in itself, but left an everlasting impress on the character of McKendree, and uprightness of conversation. An experience which vindicates itself in that way cannot be lightly put aside as of no real religious importance. . . . Call it perfect love, entire sanctification, or what you will, it is the experience in full and glorious measure of the powers of the world to come."

CHAPTER VII

A FURTHER "CLOUD OF WITNESSES"

The church is not lacking in a multitude of witnesses to the experience of holiness as a definite work of grace subsequent to regeneration. Many of the greatest leaders in the church have left the record of their testimony for all time as to the cleansing and enduement power which came to them in an epochal experience following their conversion.

George Mueller stands as one of the greatest men of prayer of modern times. Some years ago I heard Dr. Gross Alexander say: "I regard George Mueller as the greatest man of prayer since the days of the apostles." The great orphanage which he established and operated for more than half a century in answer to prayer has been well described as, "the standing miracle in the nineteenth century." The money which he spent in this work, amounting to a total of more than seven millions of dollars, came in answer to prayer. The secret of power in his wonderful life is attributed by one of his biographers to "a divine baptism" which came after his conversion. "George Mueller was converted in 1825 while a student in the University at Halle, but until 1829 he seems hardly to have known whether there be any Holy Spirit. He has graphically told us, how that in that year,

44

while staying at Tergmouth, in England, he was made acquainted with the person and office work of the Comforter, and how the blessed secret of this Spirit's guidance and illumination and enduement was made known to him. It all came to him now as a divine baptism." Mr. Mueller speaks of this experience in his own words: "In the beginning of September I returned to London, much better in body; and as to my soul the change was so great that it was like a second conversion." The Word of God came to have a new meaning to Mr. Mueller following this Pentecostal baptism, which he says was "like a second conversion." In describing the new significance of the Word of God following the baptism with the Holy Ghost, Mr. Mueller says: "The result was that the first evening I shut myself in my room, to give myself to prayer and meditation over the Scriptures, I learned more in a few hours than I had done in a period of several months previously."

One of the greatest men of the church of the last century was Rev. Charles G. Finney, whom God used to shake the world with a mighty revival of religion. Dr. Lyman Beecher declared that the great revival under Finney "was the greatest work of God and the greatest revival of religion that the world has ever seen in so short a time, one hundred thousand being reported as having connected themselves with the churches as a result of that great revival."

Mr. Finney describes his conversion in his autobiography in a manner that can leave no doubt but that he was genuinely saved. It was not long after his conversion until he came into a Pentecostal experience of mighty enduement and power. Mr. Finney's description of his experience following this conversion sounds very much like a page from the Acts of the Apostles. The description is given in the following words:

"I then received a mighty baptism of the Holy Spirit. Without any expectation of it, without ever having thought in my mind that there was such a thing for me, without any recollection that I had ever heard the thing mentioned by any person in the world, the Holy Spirit descended upon me in a manner that seemed to go through me, body and soul. I could feel the impression like a wave of electricity going through and through me. Indeed, it seemed to come in waves of liquid love; for I could not express it in any other way. It seemed like the breath of God. I can recollect distinctly that it seemed to fan me like immense wings. *No words can express the wonderful love that was shed abroad in my heart.* I wept aloud with joy and love, and I do not know but I should say I literally bellowed out the unutterable gushings of my heart. Those waves came over me, one after another, until I recollect I cried out, 'I shall die if these waves continue to pass over me.' I said, 'Lord, I cannot bear any more.' Yet f had no fear of death. . . Thus I continued until late at night. I received some sound repose. When I awoke in the morning the sun had risen and was pouring a clear light into my my room. Words cannot express the impression this sunlight made upon me. Instantly the baptism I had received the night before returned upon me in the same manner. I arose upon my knees in the bed and wept aloud for joy, and remained for some time too much overwhelmed with the baptism of the Spirit to do anything but pour out my soul to God. It seemed as if this morning's baptism was accompanied with a gentle reproof, and the Spirit seemed to say to me, 'Will you doubt? Will you doubt?' I cried, 'No; I will not doubt: I cannot doubt.' He then cleared the subject up so much to my mind that it was impossible for me to doubt that *the Spirit of God had taken possession of my soul.*"

The name of Frances E. Willard stands high in the hall of fame, among the great of the world. She perhaps contributed more to the cause of temperance and social purity than any other woman of modern times. At her death Christians of all faiths paid homage to her magnificent life, and her wonderful work for the cause of Christ and humanity. Among the last words she uttered before departing from this life were, "How beautiful to be with God!" Miss Willard has left behind a very definite testimony to the experience of holiness as having come to

her life in an epochal crisis subsequent to her regeneration. It was through the ministry of Dr.
and Mrs. Phoebe Palmer that Miss Willard was
led into the experience in the winter of 1866, in a
meeting at Evanston. Miss Willard described
the experience in her own words: "One evening,
early in their meeting, when Mrs. Palmer had
spoken with marvelous clearness and power, and
at the close those desirous of entering into the
higher Christian life had been asked to kneel at
the altar, another crisis came to me. It was not
so tremendous as the first, but it was one that
deeply left its impress on my spirit. . . *Kneel-
ing in utter self-abandonment I consecrated myself anew to God.*

"I cannot describe the deep welling of joy
that gradually possessed me. I was utterly free
from care. I was blithe as a bird that is good
for nothing except to sing. . . . The conscious,
emotional presence of Christ through the Holy
Spirit held me. I ran about upon his errands
'just for love.' Life was a halcyon day. All my
friends knew and noticed the change, and I
would not like to write down the lovely things
some of them said to me; but they did me no
harm, for I was shut in with the Lord.

"Since then I have sat at the feet of every
teacher of holiness whom I could reach; have
read their books and compared their views. I
love and reverence and am greatly drawn toward all, and never feel out of harmony with

their spirit. Wonderful uplifts come to me as I pass on—clearer views of the life of God and the soul of man. Indeed, it is the only life, and all my being sets toward it as the rivers toward the sea."

CHAPTER VIII

THE UPPER ROOM IN A LOWER ROOM

In previous chapters we have given some of the testimonies of the great leaders of the church to the experience of holiness as a definite work of grace subsequent to regeneration. While the details varied in these experiences, we found a remarkable unanimity in their testimonies to the fact that after they were saved there came a second epochal crisis in obtaining the Baptism with the Holy Ghost.

This company of witnesses to the experience of holiness is not confined to the past. A great multitude may be found in our present day in the churches, who give testimony to the blessed experience of heart purity. The experience is vital and real with them. They know whereof they speak. They would be untrue to God, and grieve the Holy Ghost, if they failed to witness to that which has taken place in their own lives.

The greatest boon to my own ministry has been, that while still a boy preacher I was led into this Canaan of Christian experience. I was converted early in childhood, and united with the Methodist Church. I was fortunate in having Christian parents, who surrounded my early life with strong, Christian influences. My father conducted the old-fashioned family altar in the home, and the entire family was always in the house of God when the circuit riders came to the community for their preaching engagements. The community of my childhood was in the Ozark hill country of Missouri.

I shall never forget the revivals held by the circuit riders during my early childhood. These men of God preached a gospel which was the power of God unto salvation. They were fearless in their denunciation of sin, and the proclamation of the coming judgment. Sinners were mightily convicted of sin. I recall seeing the mourner's bench repeatedly filled with penitent hearts, and hearing the triumphant shouts of victory of new-born souls as they prayed through to a saving knowledge of the Lord Jesus Christ.

These revival experiences had a very wholesome influence upon my life as a small child. Some of our modern teachers of Christian Education have been greatly misled about the relation of the child to a great Holy Ghost revival. Some of them even go so far as to counsel that children should not be taken to such revivals; but these same educators raise no protest to taking the children to the football game, where emotional excesses may be found on a scale far beyond anything witnessed in the old-fashioned revival of Holy Ghost religion. "Consistency, thou art a jewel!" The fact of the matter is, there is nothing our young people need more today than to come in contact with genuine revivals of religion, where the Holy Ghost is manifested in mighty convicting and saving power.

My call to the ministry came early in my teen-age, while a lad in high school. I wrestled for some time over this call. It was not my desire to be a minister, I wanted to be a lawyer. I enjoyed a debate, and was a member of more than one debating club in those days. The law appealed to me as a natural outlet for my propensities along this line. The call to the ministry was in no sense pleasing to me. The struggle in my soul extended over a period of many months. God used the story of Jonah and the whale in settling the question. If I ran from the call of God in rejecting the ministry, I had a profound conviction that somewhere along the journey of life the fish of circumstances would swallow me, as definitely as the whale swallowed Jonah. Thus an Old Testament story, the authenticity of which has been questioned by many modernists, was used as a great blessing to my soul. To me the story of Jonah and the big fish was no mere myth, but the record of an event that really happened. I am quite sure that the interpretation which some modern teachers give to this story, lifting it out of the historical setting into the realm of myth, would have had little or no influence in enabling me to yield to the call to the ministry. Having finally settled the issued by saying "yes" to God I was happy in my decision.

After completing high school I went to college, to prepare for the ministry. I entered Marvin College, a college of the Methodist Church, located at Fredericktown, Mo. During that first year, Rev. Marvin T. Haw, then pastor of the Methodist Church at Jackson, Mo., was called to hold a revival meeting in Fredericktown. His meeting was held in the Methodist Church, with the college faculty and students participating. During the days of that meeting a very godly woman came to assist in the matter of holding cottage prayer meetings, and doing personal work. Her name was Mrs. Skinner, or better known as "Sister Skinner," who, as I understand, was the first deaconess ever appointed under the Woman's Board of Methodist Episcopal Church, South. She served for many years at Centenary Church, St. Louis. Although having retired from regular appointment, she went about among the churches doing personal work, holding cottage meetings, and helped pray down the power of God upon the preacher and the people. To look into her face was to realize that she walked with her Lord in a manner above that of the ordinary Christian.

It was my good fortune to fall into one of Sister Skinner's cottage meetings. There were only five present, three preacher boys, including myself, Sister Skinner, and the host in the home where Sister Skinner was being entertained. The crowd was not large but it was a memorable meeting. The informal meeting had hardly opened when Sister Skinner asked of me a personal question. She said: "Do you believe in sanctification?" I was somewhat hesitant in my reply, saying, "I hardly know whether I do or not. I have heard many extreme things mentioned in connection with sanctification. You will have to explain to me what you mean before I can answer you." It was then a heavenly glow lit upon a face ripened with years, as I heard the simple unfolding of the significance and the meaning of this great experience. Before she finished my heart was hungry and crying out for what she was talking about. When she finished I said' "Is this what you mean by sanctification?" She said, "Yes." I replied: "Then if this is what it is, I accept it by faith here and now." She arose from her chair, crossed the room with the glow of that heavenly smile upon her face, saying, as she approached me, "Do you believe the Lord sanctifies you now?" My response was, "Yes, I *know* he does, praise the Lord!" The tidal waves of joy and glory flooded my soul. I shouted "Glory to God!"

Sister Skinner then called us to our knees in prayer, and the other two preacher-boys who were with me prayed through to the Canaan experience. This cottage meeting was not held in an Upper Room; it happened to be a lower room on the first floor. But we found there an Upper Room experience. One of the young men in college, who has since become a prominent educator, being the President of one of our state universities, said to me: "McPheeters, some of us who are your close friends are disappointed to see you take off after sanctification. But we are confident it is a matter that will soon blow over, and will not last for long." Contrary to my friend's prophecy, I have found this experience has abided through the years, growing in richness as we journey on.

In the winter of 1918 I broke down with tuberculosis in the midst of a busy pastorate in the city of St. Louis. I had an extensive involvement in both lungs, running a temperature of 103 day and night, and raising three cups of moisture per day. One of America's greatest doctors at the time told me he did not know whether I could be cured. I faced the reality of eternity. I had time to think and review my ministry in the light of perhaps going soon into the presence of God to give an account. Amid the testing of those days there was one thing I had to be thankful for above everything else, and it was this: that during my ministry I had preached and witnessed to the experience of sanctification, and in those days I renewed my covenant with God to continue the proclamation of this message even with renewed emphasis if he should in his good providence raise me from a bed of affliction, for which the best doctors held out but little hope. God touched my body and

raised me up, and I rejoice in the glorious priv-
ilege of still proclaiming this blessed message:
"The blood of Jesus Christ, His Son, cleanseth us
from all sin."

CHAPTER IX

THE TEST OF REALITY

We have presented a number of witnesses bearing a definite testimony to the experience of holiness, as having been received as an instantaneous work of grace subsequent to regeneration. These testimonies will be discounted by some on the basis that the witnesses were lacking in adequate theological discrimination. It seems apropos that at this stage of our discussion we should bring forward the testimony of some of the recognized theologians on the subject of holiness.

John Wesley won for himself world wide recognition as an authority on holiness. Olin Alfred Curtis, whose work on systematic theology has been used extensively as a text in Methodist seminaries and courses of study for Methodist preachers, says: 'Historically, Wesley had almost the same epochal relation to the doctrinal emphasis upon holiness that Luther had to the doctrinal emphasis upon justification by faith, or that Athanasius had to the doctrinal emphasis upon the deity of our Lord." Curtis believes that Wesley was a much more reliable authority on the subject of holiness than many modern teachers who try to discount his teaching on the subject. As the leader of an epochal movement Curtis says that Wesley "had at hand *quantity in data.''* In adding further comment, Curtis says: "The flaw in some of the modern discussions of Christian perfection is not so much in the reasoning as in the want of sufficient data to reason upon." No man of modern times has had a greater *"quantity in data"* to draw from than John Wesley, and few if any have had such a quantity.

John Wesley not only possessed *"quantity in data"* but he also possessed a "surety in discrimination." In making this observation Curtis says: "There are several recent scientific studies of Christian experience which would be almost priceless in value had the authors only known the difference between reality and imitation. It is possible to obtain a thousand answers to a list of questions, and have only a hundred of them with any real Christian meaning. It was just at this point that John Wesley was a master in Israel. . . . Wesley had such extraordinary spiritual insight, and such sanity in judgment, that often his most casual statement, especially in his journal, is more illuminating than many profound monographs in theology."

In a letter written from London, bearing the date of June 19, 1771, Mr. Wesley said: "Many years since I saw that 'without holiness no man shall see the Lord.' I began following after it, and inciting all with whom I had any intercourse to do the same. Ten years after, God gave me a clearer view than I had before of the way to attain this, namely, by faith in the Son of God. And immediately I declared to all, 'We are saved from sin, we are made holy, by faith.' This I testified in private, in public, in print; and God confirmed it by a thousand witnesses. I have continued to declare this for above thirty years; and God hath continued to confirm the word of his grace."   As to the method of the attainment of the experience of holiness, Wesley says: "I believe that perfection is always wrought in the soul by a simple act of faith; consequently, in an instant. But I believe a gradual work, both preceding and following that instant."

Holiness was a dominant doctrine and teaching among the early Methodists. Gilbert T. Rowe, one of the well known present day theological writers, in his book, "The Meaning of Methodism," quotes John Wesley as writing toward the end of his life these words: "Blessed be God, though we set a hundred enthusiasts aside, we are still 'compassed with a cloud of witnesses,' who have testified, and do testify, in life and in death, that perfection which I have taught these forty years!"   Dr. Rowe, in speaking of the emphasis placed by early Methodists on holiness, says: "In the early days both sinners and Christians were invited to come to the altar, the former for conversion and the latter for sanctification.   There is now in a church in England an old Methodist register, upon which the names are marked, 'seeker,' 'saved,' or 'sanctified.'   Reports of many of the early camp meetings in this country gave so many 'saved' and so many 'sanctified,' and when Asbury made his last trip through the South, the burden of his message was the instantaneous experience of entire sanctification.   Several of the old Disciples earnestly urged the preachers to preach sanctification as an instantaneous second work of grace. And yet, while this view has persisted in groups within the large branches of Methodism, and also in smaller churches which have separated from them, it has never been able to get a hold upon the general Methodist conscience."

Dr. Rowe, in making further comment, says: "Why is this?   Why has the experience, variously designated 'the second blessing,' 'entire sanctification,' 'the second work of grace,' 'the baptism of the Spirit,' and 'baptism for service.' dropped out, or rather never been able to get a general hold upon Methodism?   Because experience, the great trier of all doctrines, theories and suppositions, has found that the profession of entire sanctification as an instantaneous work does not stand the test of reality.   As a general theory it does not work.   People who profess it soon find that they are subject to the same temptations that Christians generally have, and members who are 'entirely sanctified' do not display greater wisdom or piety than those who are not."

Dr. Rowe faces the issue squarely as to the teaching of John Wesley and the early Methodists concerning holiness as an instantaneous epochal experience coming subsequent to regeneration. He does not fall into the blunder of some eminent modern writers in spending much time and effort in an endeavor to prove that Mr. Wesley was mixed up in his teaching, and taught two separate theories concerning holiness, and that in the latter years of his life he weakened in his emphasis on holiness|. Dr. Rowe's statements also leave no doubt as to the position of the early Methodist leaders. The records are clear, as in the case of Francis Asbury, that holiness as an instantaneous work of grace subsequent to regeneration, was a dominant doctrine in the preaching and teaching of the early Methodist leaders.

We are, however, surprised when Dr. Rowe says: " . . . entire sanctification as an instantaneous work does not stand the test of reality." He quoted Mr. Wesley as writing toward the end of his life: "We are still 'compassed about with a cloud of witnesses;' " as to the reality of sanctification as an instantaneous work, and then follows within a few paragraphs with his own statement: " . . . entire sanctification as an instantaneous work does not stand the test of reality." When evaluating the statements of Mr. Wesley and Dr. Rowe, it seems only fair to raise the question: "Who has 'at hand *quantity in data,'* for forming the more accurate conclusion, Mr. Wesley or Dr. Rowe?" We believe that Mr. Wesley had "at hand *quantity in data,*" which would give his statement precedence in most any court where evidence is weighed.

If "entire sanctification as an instantaneous work does not stand the test of reality" what about 'a cloud of witnesses' whose testimony cannot with any degree of fairness be questioned, which is to the fact that this experience does stand the test of reality? What about Francis Asbury and William McKendree? What about the host of other Methodist bishops who have witnessed to this experience standing the "test of reality?" What about Frances E. Willard? What about General William Booth and the Salvation Army? What about Dwight L. Moody, and Charles G. Finney, who both witnessed to being baptized with the Holy Ghost subsequent to regeneration? What about Lizzie H. Glide, who has been properly designated as "the most philanthropic woman of world Methodism?" Mrs. Glide has told the writer repeatedly that her sanctification as an instantaneous work of grace following her regeneration, was the beginning of her world-wide program of Christian philathropy. Until these testimonies along with an innumerable host of others are invalidated, the statement that " . . . entire sanctification as an instantaneous work does not stand the test of reality" must remain challenged. .

CHAPTER X

A SOUND PSYCHOLOGICAL BASIS

We have introduced the testimony of some prominent theologians concerning the experience of holiness as a definite epochal experience subsequent to regeneration. One of the theologians mentioned was Olin Alfred Curtis whose work on systematic theology has been used as a text in a number of Methodist seminaries and has also been included in courses of study for Methodist preachers. Dr. Curtis is very clear in his statements concerning the teaching of John Wesley on the subject. In giving his interpretation of John Wesley's teaching he says: "According to John Wesley, a sinner has three things the matter with him: First, he is guilty; second, he is morally powerless; and, third, his inherent and inherited disposition is wrong. Or, as I would say, the individuality is out of harmony with the ideal of the moral person. When a sinner is justified the guilt is cancelled. When he is regenerated he receives a nucleus of power, not enough 'to fight it to a standstill.' In Christian perfection, there is no such fight with the disposition, 'no civil war at all' for the wrong impulse never enters the consciousness as motive."

Dr. Curtis gives a concrete illustration to illustrate the meaning and significance of holiness as taught by John Wesley. In presenting the illustration he says: "It will help us all probably, if I can give a concrete illustration of Wesley's view. Here is a man, a Christian preacher now, who has from infancy been naturally jealous. He is not only converted, but is a noble Christian man, ready to sacrifice for his Lord, and equally ready to serve his brethren. But he is still jealous in disposition. Yesterday he heard another preacher's sermon receive large commendation and like an uprush of mercury in the heat, that old feeling of jealousy rose into consciousness. His volition, his personality, had no more to do with it than his will had to do with the coming on of night. But the moment our preacher realizes that he is jealous he makes Christian battle, and forces the disposition back, back into its cave. Now, we have here an exceedingly strange psychological situation, for the man's struggle is plainly Christian in its revelation of the moral ideal, and yet the struggle reveals a motive-life which no Christian ought to have at all. Or, we can say this: The victory is truly that of a Christian man—but as a Christian man he should have been without the possibility of that kind of a battle. Now comes a pivotal inquiry. As our preacher grows what does his growth in grace accomplish? According to Wesley, the growth does not affect the inherent disposition of jealousy at all; but it does bring the regenerate man himself to a more potent attitude, both of intolerance toward the disposition and of trust toward Jesus Christ. With this more potent personal attitude the man dares to believe that his Lord can and will take that jealousy, and every wrong disposition out of his life. In full, simple faith he asks Christ to do it; and precisely as when he was converted, it is all done at one stroke. Now what is the man's condition? On the one hand, he never is conscious of jealousy.   Rather does he spontaneously rejoice in another man's success.   On the other hand, he never comes to self-consciousness without being filled, like the prodigality of a freshet, with the love of God.   This, as I understand him, is what John Wesley means by the conquest of inbred sin through supreme love.   And if there is one man here to whom Wesley's view of inbred sin suggests no reality, no point in kindred experience, he most surely is to be regarded as extremely fortunate."

After giving this analysis of John Wesley's view of Christian perfection, Dr. Curtis raises the question as to whether or not Mr. Wesley's view will stand the test of scriptural argument in the light of modern scholarship.   In speaking on this point Dr. Curtis says: "Is there, though, for this Wesleyan doctrine of Christian perfection any support in biblical theology?   In Wesley's day there was such an arbitrary and fragmentary and superficial use of Scripture, even by the finest scholars, that many students have

gained the impression, if not the belief, that the
scriptural argument for Christian perfection
cannot endure the test of our modern method of
studying the Bible. I am certain that the test
can be endured." After making this statement,
Dr. Curtis gives several pages to presenting the
scriptural grounds for Christian perfection.

Dr. Curtis believes that Christian perfection
also has a sound psychological basis. In speaking of the psychological basis of Christian perfection, he says: "As we have seen, the motive-
life of a regenerate man is organized about the
motive of *loyalty to Christ*. The motive of loyalty is not a simple motive, but is made up of two
elements, one of love and the other of duty. At
rare moments these two elements are in self-consciousness with equal force, but usually the sense
of duty is paramount. The regenerate man, in
any typical situation, is seeking to do his duty.
His common remark is: 'I will be true! I will not
deny my Lord.' This loyalty is very different
from the loyalty of the moralist; and for two
reasons, namely, it is loyalty to a person, and it
is rooted in the enthusiasm of a positive personal
affection. And yet the Christian loyalty has
some of the same psychological weakness which
renders morality so ineffective. Duty always
implies a conflict, a civil war. The sense of the
ought is, like a bugle, intended to call the person
into battle. And while this moral battle is great,
it is less than the highest mood. You will see

what I mean, if you think of a home where husband, wife, parents, children are ever trying to do their duty to each other. What a dreadful home that would be! Not one day with the simple, rejoicing impulse of dominant love.

"In personal holiness this motive of loyalty is transformed into the simple motive of pure love. There remains all of the ethical quality of duty, for the new supreme love is a moral love; but 'the whip of the ought' is gone. The holy person does not do things because it is his duty to do them, but *because he loves to do them*. But note this closely, the important thing here, psychologically, is not the vastness of the love (that is a matter of endless growth), but simply that the love *entirely occupies the self-conscious mood*. Whenever the person comes to self-consciousness it is crammed with love to the very edges. Thus, there is a perfect personal organism, because all of the man's motivity is nothing but love in a variety of shapes. In the man's personal life there is no antagonism, no civil war whatever. He may be tempted, as we shall see, but he cannot be tempted by his own inorganic condition, by his own depravity."

Dr. Curtis lays emphasis upon the crisis by which the regenerate enter into the experience of Christian perfection. He recognizes, of course, a growth preceding the crisis and a growth following it. He says: "But is personal holiness obtained gradually by earnest endeavor. Looking at it in the most comprehensive way, our answer should be in the affirmative; for the crisis itself is profoundly involved in all that has led up to it."

Following this statement concerning the growth preceding the crisis, Dr. Curtis magnifies "Wesley's emphasis upon the ultimate stroke." Concerning the importance of this "ultimate stroke," he says: "And yet John Wesley's emphasis upon the ultimate stroke is exceedingly important. For there is a great difference between the last phase of the regenerate life and the first phase of the life of supreme love. As it is only in the latter case that the motive of loyalty *entirely* loses the note of duty; only in the latter case that love absolutely fills self-consciousness to its rim; so only in the latter case that all the wrong motives of disposition are exhausted.

"But the question has been asked, 'Why, on the principle of your discussion of motivity, may a regenerate man, with his motive of loyalty, not fight his way into personal holiness?' My answer is this: To exhaust all wrong motive by a sheer negative fight would require more time than belongs to our earthly life; and even if there were time enough the victory would exalt the element of duty and not the element of love in the motive of loyalty. What we are after is so to escape sin as to escape the bondage of conscience itself, and, like God himself, live the life of moral love."

CHAPTER XI

Many and varied are the definitions given to the terms used in the interpretation of Scriptural holiness. No little of the misunderstandings which have arisen among Christians upon this subject have come from a lack of uniformity in the definition of terms. The terms used to designate Scriptural holiness, as interpreted by John Wesley, have been widely misunderstood by a large group of Christian people. Much of the prejudice and opposition against the experience has arisen from a perverted understanding of the terms used in its interpretation. We can hardly hope to set forth a series of definitions to which exceptions will not be taken.

One of the sanest and best sets of definitions has been compiled by Rev. Daniel Steele, D. D., in the preface of his book: "Love Enthroned." Dr. Steele was, for a number of years, Professor of New Testament Greek in Boston University. His definitions are as follows:

DEFINITIONS

Much controversy on the subject of Christian Perfection has arisen from the use of terms having various meanings. It is our purpose to notify the reader whenever we pass from one significance of a term to another.

1. Holy. (1.) Set apart to the service of God.

Applied to persons and things.

(2.) Morally pure, free from all stain of sin. Persons.

(3.) In the New Testament the original Greek word is used technically to designate all justified believers, and is translated by the word "saints" or holy ones.

2. Holiness. The state of, (1.) Consecration to God.

(2.) Moral purity.

3. Sanctify. (1.) To hallow, to consecrate to religious uses. "I sanctify myself."—Jesus.

(2.) To make pure, to cleanse from moral defilement. "The very God of peace sanctify you wholly."—St. Paul.

(3.) Sanctified—In the New Testament used technically to designate the justified.

4. Sanctification. Holiness: the act of making holy.

5. The Moral Law. (1.) Unwritten; the sense of moral obligation felt within.

(2.) Written; the Decalogue, with its (a) prohibitions; (b) Precepts. Also the two tables, prescribing (a) Duties to God; (b) Duties to man.

6. Sin. (1.) *Actual*. A willful transgression of the known law of God. Sin of commission, disobedience to a pro-

hibition. Sin of omission, neglect of a precept. "Sin is the transgression of the law." St. John.

Sin. (2) *Original* or *inbred*—often without any adjective, and always in the singular number—a state, not an act. Native corruption of the moral nature derived from Adam's apostasy. A lack of conformity to the moral law. Under the remedial dispensation it involves no guilt till approved by the free agent and its remedy is rejected. It is intensified by acts of sin of which it is the source. "All unrighteousness is sin." St. John.

7. Perfection. As applied to man. (1.) *Legal* or *Adamic*. Entire conformity to the moral law. "I have seen an end of all perfection, (for) thy law is exceeding broad."—David.

(2) *Celestial*. The complete restoration of both soul and body in the glorified state after the resurrection. "Not as though I had already attained, either were already perfect."—St. Paul.

(3) *Ideal* or *Absolute*. The combination of all conceivable excellences in the highest degree. Ascribed only to God, and not to beings capable of endless progress. "I am perfect."—God. "If I say I am perfect, it shall also prove me perverse."—Job.

(4) *Evangelical* or *Christian*. The loving God
with all our heart, mind, soul, and strength,
and our neighbor as ourselves, with the complete exclusion of every feeling contrary to
pure love. "Love is the fulfilling of the law."
—St. Paul. "The bond of perfectness;" the
sum total of the virtues.—St. Paul, translated by Bengel. "There is a twofold perfection, the perfection of the work, and that of
the workman."—Bishop Hopkins. The former is legal, the later is evangelical perfection, which is nothing but inward sincerity,
uprightness of heart toward God, although
there may be many imperfections and defects intermingled.

We believe that a careful examination of
these terms will reveal that there is a remarkable conformity to Scriptural teaching. Dr.
Steele points out the two-fold meaning of the
word "sanctify," and the technical use of the
term to designate the justified in the New Testament. It is well that we should understand clearly the two-fold meaning of the term relative to
consecration to religious uses and to cleansing
from moral defilement. Much is said about consecration in many of our religious gatherings,
but very little emphasis is placed upon the necessity of cleansing from moral depravity. It is
for this reason that many of our consecration
services fall short of the epochal crisis which

brings the believer into the Canaan experience
of perfect love.

It is important that, under the heading of
sin, we clearly comprehend the two-fold nature
of sin as manifested in depravity spoken of as
original or inbred sin, and also in the actual or
overt act of sin.   Both of these phases of the
manifestation of sin demand a remedy.   Our
actual sins demand forgiveness.   Our depravity,
or inbred sin, demands cleansing.   I heard a
prominent preacher contend in the pulpit that
our depravity could never be cleansed.   His con-
tention was that it might be subdued, and even
bound and put down in the basement of the
house, but that it could never be put out of the
house.   The all-sufficient atonement of Jesus
made upon the cross was not only for the forgiveness of the overt acts of sin, but also for the
cleansing of the corruption of the moral nature
in which the overt acts of sin find their roots.

One of the most widely misunderstood terms
as applied to Christian experiences is the term
"perfection."   It is important that we understand the different phases of the use of the term
in the Bible.   Dr. Steele sets forth the meaning
of the term under four phases.   It is the last
phase of the term which we have in mind when
speaking of Christian perfection.   This perfection is described as, "loving God with all our
heart, mind, soul, strength, and our neighbor as
ourself, with the complete exclusion of every

feeling contrary to pure love." Is there anything unreasonable in such an experience? Can
anything be more desirable than this? Is anything more scriptural? This is a perfection
"which is nothing but inward sincerity, and uprightness of heart toward God, although there
may be many imperfections and defects intermingled." There will be many imperfections of
judgment and mistakes on the part of those who
love God with all the heart, mind, soul and
strength. But such imperfections are not in-
compatible with a pure heart which loves God
supremely. This perfection which involves the
loving God with all the heart, mind, soul, and
strength is a goal unto which every Christian
should strive to attain. Such a goal seems to be
clearly uplifted in the questions propounded by
the Bishop to every Methodist preacher entering
the Annual Conference. The questions are:

"Are you going on to perfection? Do you
expect to be made perfect in love in this life? Are
you groaning after it?"

CHAPTER XII

The present stage of our discussion of Christian perfection hinges around the testimony of eminent theologians. Dr. Wilbur F. Tillett, who for many years was Dean of the School of Theology at Vanderbilt University, is the author of, "Studies in Christian Doctrine, Pertaining to the Spiritual Life." This book has been widely used as a text for Methodist preachers, having been in the Course of Study for many years. Dr. Tillett differs with a number of the other great Methodist theologians in his interpretation of John Wesley's view of sanctification. Dr. Tillett holds the view that that element of the sinful nature commonly spoken of as the "root of sin," or "inbred sin," which many believe is removed in an epochal experience subsequent to regeneration, is removed at the time of regeneration. He believes that the acts of surrender and consecration are involved in one work of grace.

Dr. Tillett is frank to admit that if sin still remains in the believer in the form of a "sinful nature," "the being of sin," "evil feelings," or "evil tempers," then a second definite work of grace is needed. In discussing this point Dr. Tillett says: "If it be true that sin is left in the regenerate after their conversion, and if that residue of sin does include 'sins' as those above enumerated, it is quite evident that a second radical and instantaneous work of grace is as much needed for the full and complete salvation of penitent believers as such a work was needed in the first instance when they were justified and regenerated." We believe that the verdict of Christian experience across the centuries is to the fact that the Christian believer discovers an inner warfare after his conversion, which speaks of the necessity of that "instantaneous work of grace" to which Dr. Tillett refers and which he admits as a necessity, if such sin as 'evil feelings' and 'evil tempers' are manifest.

Dr. Tillett is of the opinion that John Wesley was somewhat confused in his thinking on the subject of Christian Perfection. He believes that Mr. Wesley held two views upon the subject. Concerning the first view of Mr. Wesley Dr. Tillett says: "The first view is that which regards every child of God who measures up to the ideal state of a justified and regenerate believer as 'perfect' in the New Testament sense of that term." Concerning the second view he says: "The second view of Christian perfection identifies it with sanctification, and is based on the idea that to be a truly justified and regenerate child of God is not in itself alone to possess Christian perfection." He also speaks of this second view by heading the paragraph of his discussion with the words: "Entire sanctification an instantaneous experience subsequent to regeneration."

Theologians equally as eminent as Dr. Tillett have not discovered in Mr. Wesley's writings the confused thinking on the question of Christian Perfection which Dr. Tillett thinks he has discovered. Some of these theologians have already been quoted, and others will be quoted further on.

In the conclusion of his book Dr. Tillett has a paragraph bearing the title, "A Possible Basis of Agreement." In this paragraph he says: 'Recognizing two distinct theories of entire sanctification as involved in his writings, let us stress the point which he admitted as possible that — 'instantaneous sanctification,' though generally occurring later, may take place at conversion—and we will thereby obliterate all necessary and radical difference between his two theories."

It is significant that even Dr. Tillett admits the predominant view of John Wesley was "instantaneous sanctification" subsequent to regeneration.

While Dr. Tillett urges salvation from both the guilt of sin and the being of sin at conversion, he makes this rather interesting statement: "If it be found that any one who thinks he has been converted comes to the consciousness of sin in himself of any kind—'inbred sin,' sins of temper, pride, self-will, etc.—let us insist that he needs, and must have at once, a further radical and instantaneous work of grace in order to be saved from all sin; and let that work be called by any Scripture name that may suggest itself to any one as most proper." It is very interesting indeed to read such a statement after wading through the major thesis of Dr. Tillett to the effect that sanctification is obtained at conversion. If we follow his instruction relative to urging believers who have the consciousness of "inbred sin," sins of temper, pride, self-will, etc., to seek an instantaneous work of grace subsequent to regeneration, how many believers would be fit subjects for such exhortation? Again we bring forward the verdict of Christian experience across the pathway of the centuries. Let that experience be heeded by the Church in the light of Dr. Tillett's exhortation, and we will begin the proclamation of a definite Pentecost for believers from every pulpit in the land. One thing is very clear in Dr. Tillett's discussion. While contending for sanctification at conversion, he admits the possibility of conversion without sanctification; and that sanctification may come as a work subsequent to regeneration.

The sin that lies at the door of the church today is the fact that little or nothing is being said about sanctification. We have multitudes of devout people in our churches who are very much like those disciples at Ephesus who answered the inquiry of Paul concerning their baptism with the Holy Ghost with the statement: "We have not so much as heard whether there be any Holy Ghost." I heard one of the greatest preachers in Methodism recently make the statement: "I was a Methodist preacher for twenty years before I dared to study in earnest the Bible teaching concerning the baptism with the Holy Ghost." This man has held the highest official positions within the gift of the Church, excepting the Episcopacy only. Today he is very pronounced in his teaching concerning the experience of Pentecost coming subsequent to regeneration.

The lack of power in the modern church is apparent on every hand. The holiness and faith movements today are outstrippping the major denominations in their missionary and evangelistic programs, on a comparative basis of membership and financial strength.

An interesting editorial in a recent edition of the Christian Evangelist, the national weekly of the Disciples of Christ, calls attention to the spread of Holiness churches in the United States. The editorial says: "Among the economically depressed in the city and country slums holiness bodies—or those loosely akin—are functioning widely. These congregations are by no means won by modernism; they are thoroughly fundamentalist, and they probably form the most rapidly growing American religious group." This editorial statement corroborates the findings of Roger Babson in his recent nation-wide religious survey on church attendance. Mr. Babson says that the Holiness churches in the United States are the only ones among the Protestants who have not suffered a marked decline in church attendance in recent years. The editorial referred to concludes with this significant statement: "What we need in our religion is a little less gentility, a little less respectability, a little less comfort and security, and a little more of the dynamite of the Christian gospel. America and the world are in sore need of a non-genteel religion." What think ye of such a statement coming from the Disciples of Christ? Such a statement ought to be an awakening note to modern day Methodists.

Methodism again needs to be fired with the flaming message of holiness which characterized the preaching of Wesley, Fletcher, Asbury, and McKendree. Let us again recapture this glorious truth and blessed experience, and Methodism can shake the world with the Great Awakening for which devout souls everywhere are praying. Unless we recapture this heritage future generations will read the name, "Ichabod," written over our portals.

CHAPTER XIII

A LITTLE LEAVEN, LEAVENING THE LUMP

Theologians and church historians stand in agreement in their testimony to the fact that the early Methodists gave large emphasis to the doctrine of Christian Perfection. Humphrey Lee, in his recent book, "John Wesley and Modern Religion," introduces chapter eight of the book with the statement: "Wesley's most distinctive doctrine is unquestionably that of Christian Perfection." He further says in the same chapter: " 'Without holiness no man can see the Lord' was Wesley's uncompromising slogan." In the same chapter Dr. Lee quotes a statement of John Wesley, made in 1767, in which he summarizes his thoughts on Christian Perfection: "I believe this perfection is always wrought in the soul by a simple act of faith; consequently in an instant. But I believe a gradual work both preceding and following that incident. As to the time—I believe this instant generally is the instant of death, the moment before the soul leaves the body; but I believe it may be ten, twenty or forty years before. I believe it is usually many years after justification; but that it may be within five years or five months after it, I know no conclusive argument to the contrary." Dr. Lee further says: "As to the origin and developments of his doctrine of Christian Perfection, Wesley had much to say. If it were possible, it would be better to reprint 'A Plain Account of Christian Perfection' which he wrote in 1765, and printed the next year."

If "the most distinctive doctrine" of John Wesley was "unquestionably that of Christian Perfection," what is the most distinctive doctrine of the Methodists of the present day? We believe that the doctrine of Christian Perfection was vitally related to the great Wesleyan revival, and we further believe that it will be vitally related to the next great revival when it comes. The Wesleyan doctrine of Christian Perfection had a vital relation to the great revival under Moody which shook two continents. Dr. Richard E. Day, in "Bush Aglow," a centenary biography of Dwight L. Moody, calls our attention to the fact that it was two Free Methodist women who were the human instruments God used to lead Moody to seek and obtain the baptism of the Holy Ghost, after he had become a national figure as a Christian leader. It was in 1871 that these two Free Methodist women, who were exponents in life and testimony of Wesley's doctrine of perfect love, approached Mr. Moody relative to a deeper experience for himself. The approach by these devout women was at first resented, but later was followed by conviction, which conviction resulted in his seeking and obtaining the baptism of the Holy Ghost for which his soul hungered. It was after 1871 that Moody was used in the great revivals which stirred the whole of England and America, and shed an influence which girdled the globe.

Careful observers of the present moral chaos in American life are pretty well agreed that the only hope of America is a revival of religion. Roger Babson, the noted statistician, has issued many statements to the effect that a revival of religion is America's only hope. In a recent magazine article he states that any revival of prosperity in our economic life in the United States cannot endure unless we have a revival of religion.

If the preaching of holiness on the part of John Wesley and his followers produced a revival in his day, we believe that the same gospel will bring a revival in our day. The church must again be called to the Upper Room. She herself must come to Pentecost before she can expect to reach the world in a large way. Methodism of the present day has neglected her birthright. She has attempted to substitute many things for that holiness of heart and life which characterized the preaching, teaching and living of the early Methodists. Many have come to regard the Wesleyan teaching of perfect love as an experience subsequent to regeneration, as antiquated and out of date. Some writers are speaking of the Wesleyan doctrine of holiness as a thing that has "exploded." These writers have failed to evaluate the leaven of spiritual power

on the part of a vast multitude, who, in these
modern times, stand as living witnesses to the
sanctifying grace of our Lord Jesus Christ.
They fail to take into account such persons as
those obscure Free Methodist women who led
Moody to his Pentecost. They fail to make any
adequate estimate of those churches and movements today which are characterized by the
preaching of sanctification. There is a vast
army of people in Methodism who enjoy the experience of perfect love. Suppose we eliminated
all these members from Methodist churches.
Then also suppose we eliminate the Salvation
Army, along with a group of smaller churches
who emphasize the Wesleyan teaching of Holiness. I dare say if this great spiritual force
should be suddenly subtracted from American
Christianity, some of our brethren who are writing about the Holiness Movement having "exploded" would suddenly reverse their views, and
divert their writing about something else having
"exploded" rather than the Holiness Movement.
The fact of the matter is, the *substitutes* for holiness on which the church has depended in these
modern times, *have* "exploded." The explosion
of these substitutes are quite manifest in the
present spiritual apostasy so widely manifest
throughout the land.

The Pastoral Address of the Centennial Conference of American Methodism, held in Balti-
more, December, 1884, and composed of dele-

gates from eight branches of the Methodist family, contained the following paragraph on holiness: "We remind you, brethren, that the mission of Methodism is to promote holiness. Holiness is the fulness of life, the crown of the soul, the joy and strength of the church. It is not a sentiment, nor an emotion, but a principle inwrought in the heart, the culmination of God's work in us, followed by a consecrated life. In all the borders of Methodism this doctrine is preached, and the experience of sanctification is urged. We beseech you, brethren, stand by your standards on this subject. Our founders rightly interpreted the mind of the Spirit, and gave us the truth as it is in Jesus. Let us not turn from them to follow strange lights, but rather let us believe their testimony, follow their example, seek purity of heart by faith in the cleansing blood, and then, in the steady line of consecrated living, 'go on to perfection.'"

When we recognize the fact that we have fallen upon a day when we have multiplied thousands of "zero churches" (by zero church we mean a church having no additions on profession of faith for an entire year) in the United States, it is time to ask seriously the question, "Have we not come to a day when we 'follow strange lights?'" There were 2,264 of these zero churches reported in Southern Methodism during 1936. Some of the other larger denominations have reported zero churches far in excess of this number in Southern Methodism.

The time is undoubtedly at hand when the urgent need is to marshall all the spiritual forces of this nation for a great revival. We believe that the foundation of the coming revival is to be found in those great doctrines and experiences which characterized the preaching of our fathers, and the most distinctive of these doctrines in the great Wesleyan revival was "unquestionably that of Christian Perfection."

CHAPTER XIV

OBTAINABLE IN THIS LIFE

Holiness is an inescapable subject in Methodist theology. John Wesley believed that the remaining sin in the believer's heart, designated by such terms as carnality, "roots of bitterness" and inbred sin, was taken out of the heart through the cleansing blood of Christ in sanctification. Humphrey Lee, in his book, "John Wesley and Modern Religion," in speaking of Wesley's view of remaining sin in the believer's heart, says: "Wesley believed that this remaining sin was inbred sin, the fallen nature inherited from Adam."

This doctrine of sanctification for the heart of the believer, which was so prominent in the teaching and preaching of the early Methodists, has become "the missing link" in wide circles of present day Methodism. Perhaps many of our preachers and teachers have come to believe that such men as John Wesley, Adam Clarke, John Fletcher, and Francis Asbury, were mistaken in their interpretation of this great experience. It is quite interesting to note how some modern writers sidestep the issue with explanations and interpretations, which really rob the Wesleyan doctrine of sanctification of its vitality, so far as its practical realization is concerned in our modern day church life. Some, no doubt, labor under the opinion that the Wesleyan doctrine of sanctification is contradicted by the acid test of modern philosophy.   There are still others who feel that the doctrine meets insuperable obstacles in the human body, and still others feel that it is contrary to revelation found in God's Word.

Henry C. Sheldon, for many years professor in Boston University, is the author of "System of Christian Doctrine" which has been used as a text in theological seminaries, and the course of study for Methodist preachers.   Dr. Sheldon, who has been regarded as a profound thinker in high scholastic circles is of the opinion that the objections commonly raised to the doctrine of sanctification for believers are not valid.

In speaking of the objections commonly raised to the experience of sanctification for the believer, Dr. Sheldon says: "Can this goal be reached in the present life?   In other words, can a man advance here to a state which may be described negatively as free from sin, and positively as under the complete dominion of love— a state in which the moral disposition is pure and normal through and through, and conduct fails to be ideal in all respects only through unavoidable creatively limitations?   It must be granted that observation teaches us that the period of earthly discipline is in general all too short to consummate in this sense the work of sanctification.   But, on the other hand, where is the warrant for assuming that such a consummation is strictly impossible? Philosophy certainly does not afford it, that is, a philosophy that is consummate with Christian principles. It cannot be said that the body is an insuperable obstacle to entire sanctification, for Christian truth does not allow that there is any essential sense in matter. If there is, then, any insuperable obstacle, it must be in the spirit. The human spirit is indeed finite, fallible and infirm; but not one of these qualities stands in necessary opposition to holiness. As for the sinful bias by which it is affected, who can say on grounds of reason that it is beyond remedy within the limits of earthly life? Great moral transformations are wrought in very brief intervals of time. Who then, is authorized to affirm that it is beyond the comprehension of God's remedial agency to completely sanctify a soul before death.

"A rational warrant for denying the possibility of entire sanctification in this life being thus wanting, the ground of denial must be found, if discovered at all, in revelation. It must be proved that the Scriptures teach that it is outside of the divine ability or the divine purpose to consummate the sanctification of any subject of grace before the article of death. Calvinists are hindered, of course, by their postulate from assuming that it is beyond the divine ability to do this, and non-Calvinists must needs despair of sustaining this assumption from the Scriptures, in the face of such words as those of Paul, which describe God as 'Able to do exceeding abundantly above all that we ask or think.' It remains then to deduce from the Scriptures that it is outside of the divine purpose or no part of the divine economy to bring any one to the point of entire sanctification in this life. But who has ever made a deduction of this sort which has even the appearance of legitimacy? Various passages show, indeed, that every man has unmistakable occasion to include himself in the ranks of sinners when his life is taken as a whole. Not one of these however, gives the faintest indication that its author meant to teach that in no case can sin be entirely put away before the separation of soul and body. Take for example, this declaration of John: 'If we say we have no sin, we deceive ourselves, and the truth is not in us.' What an eccentricity of exegesis to suppose that this teaching is a necessary continuance in sin, when the next verse reads, 'If we confess our sins, he is faithful and just to forgive us our sins, and to cleanse us from all unrighteousness.' "

Dr. Sheldon closes his discussion of the possibility of sanctification for the believer in this life with these interesting words:

"The New Testament gives no grounds for supposing that there is such an absolute contrast between the conditions of the heavenly life and those of Christian life in this world that sin must be entirely alien to the one, and inevitable to the other. In the absence of such a contrast, the command, instructions, and prayers which look to entire sanctification or perfect love, carry a certain presumption that the state which these terms define is of possible attainment in this life. It must be confessed, however, that it stands forth as an exceedingly high ideal. Any one who understands all that it implies will despair of its possibility, save as his heart is quickened by a large and intense faith in the marvelous power of divine grace."

CHAPTER XV

SIDE-STEPPING THE ISSUE

The doctrine of sanctification as a second definite work of grace subsequent to regeneration as taught by Wesley, Fletcher, Watson and other early Methodists, has not been lacking in verification, both in Christian experience and the testimony of a host of profound, scholarly thinkers. It has been unfortunate for the church in these modern times to abandon in a large measure the glorious heritage which made Methodism great in the beginning. In some instances we abandon our heritage for the sake of prestige with the world, but any prestige gained in such a compromise has in no way added to our spiritual glory and power. In fact, we believe that many of the leading denominations are today regretting the fact that Methodism has lost in such a large measure the dominant note of emphasis upon "Scriptural holiness" which characterized her in the beginning.

My attention has been recently called to a statement by a prominent Bishop of the Episcopal Church, made before a gathering of Christian workers in the South. The Bishop is reported having said: "We Episcopalians are trying to recover something of that spiritual power and heritage which the modern Methodists have forsaken." One of the most prominent men in the Baptist denomination, who is an author of international note, said to me recently: "I am becoming more and more interested in the doctrine of holiness which was preached by the early Methodists. I am convinced that the church must have something akin to what the early Methodists called sanctification and perfect love, if we are to have a revival in the modern church."

Methodism has an opportunity to lead the world in another spiritual awakening if she can but recover her lost heritage which made her the most powerful evangelistic force of modern times. But we can never recover this heritage by side-stepping the issue of holiness of heart for the believer, obtained through a definite act of faith, culminating a complete and entire consecration. A prominent presiding elder of the Methodist Church has made the statment: "The Methodists of modern times have been bootlegging holiness." This is rather a crude statement, but as a matter of fact, there is much truth in it. We have tried to make the world believe that we were still preaching and teaching holiness as did our fathers, but the world knows better. We have tried to tone down the teaching of the early Methodist fathers to suit the so-called modern age in which we live; but this toning down process has brought us no great victories. It has, instead brought us many a defeat.

Methodists need make no apologies for the doctrine of sanctification as taught by the early fathers. There is no need of toning down or compromising on the ground of the pride of scholarship. Just as great an array of theologians and scholars who have believed and taught sanctification as a second definite work of grace can be produced as those scholars and theologians who have not so interpreted the teachings of the Scripture concerning holiness. Dr. John Miley, the well known writer and theologian of the Methodist Episcopal Church, says: "We admit an instant partial sanctification and regeneration, and therefore may admit the possibility of an entire sanctification. Such a view of sanctification does not mean that there need be no preparation for its attainment. The necessity for a preparation is uniformly held even by such as hold strongly the second blessing view. . . . . Let it be recalled that the question here is not the maturity of the Christian life, but the purification of the nature. For the attainment of the former there must be growth,—and growth requires time. But while the subjective purification may be progressively wrought, it is not subject to the law of growth it is so thoroughly the work of God that it may be quickly wrought."

Bishop John J. Tigert, of the Methodist Episcopal Church, South, who was recognized as a great writer and thinker, made some very thought-provoking statements concerning the

Methodist doctrine of perfect love, while Book Editor, and Editor of the Methodist Review, before his elevation to the episcopacy. In an issue of the Methodist Review, 1894, he said: "Methodism has a doctrine of perfect love or Christian perfection as clearly defined and as continuously and consistently held as her doctrines of justification and regeneration. . . . In our humble judgment, the doctrine can be shown to be not only Methodistically but scripturally, psychologically, and experimentally sound. On the four pillars of scripture, psychology, Methodism, and experience, the doctrine has always reposed securely. The onslaughts of those who claim that the whole work of entire sanctification is accomplished in regeneration (Crane, Boland and others), and of those who claim the necessary ineradicability of our sinful natures, while we abide in the flesh (Mudge and others) —though each of these positions is the annihilation of the other—have not yet overturned the doctrine of Methodism. The opponents oscillate in polar vibrations from the extremes of perfect love in regeneration to that of the indestructibility of fleshliness, or the carnal mind, but do not disturb the serenity of those who abide under the equatorial sun whose tropical fervor melts all into the harmonious truth and gentle tenderness of perfect love . . . . Almost every one of Paul's epistles, like all the early Methodist disciples, has imbedded somewhere in it a little tract on Christian perfection."

CHAPTER XVI

CONSECRATED AND CLEANSED

The major religious groups recognize the validity of the Scriptural statement: "Without holiness no man shall see the Lord." They differ, however, in their interpretations as to the time and place this experience may be obtained. The Roman Catholics believe that holiness, which is a requisite for entrance into heaven, is obtained through purgatorial fires after death. The majority of the Calvinistic wing of Christian believers hold that this experience is obtained in the article of death. A distinctive doctrine of Methodism has been that holiness may be obtained as a definite experience in this life.

During the early years of her history the Methodists were very pronounced in their interpretation of holiness as an experience obtained in a second definite work of grace subsequent to regeneration. Methodist teaching to this effect was quite universal in Methodist churches until about the middle of the last century. An examination of the record of the spiritual power and the rapid growth of Methodism during that period, in no way reflects upon this distinctive doctrine of Methodism. No church since the days of the apostles enjoyed a greater manifestation of apostolic power and spiritual fervor than the Methodist people of

that period of her history, when sanctification
as a second definite work of grace was proclaimed from her pulpits in the power of the Spirit.
Dr. Parkes Cadman has observed that the Methodist circuit riders and exhorters in the early
period of Methodist history more nearly ap-
proximated apostolic inspiration than anything
the church has known since the days of the apostles.

During this period of Methodist history,
when the Wesleyan doctrine of sanctification
was given large emphasis, the growth of the
church was very remarkable. It was not uncommon in those days for the Methodist Church
to show a net increase in a single year far in excess of the combined increase of all the major
Methodist bodies at the present time. The net
increase for the year 1843 was well over one
hundred thousand.

The decline in emphasis upon the Wesleyan doctrine of sanctification as an epochal experience subsequent to regeneration began about
the middle of the last century. From that period
we find varying interpretations of the experience of holiness among Methodist leaders, which
in no way added to the spiritual fervor and power enjoyed by the Methodists of the earlier
period, when the Wesleyan view was the commonly accepted doctrine. During this latter
period of Methodist history, outstanding leaders
have challenged the doctrine of sanctification as

preached and taught by the early Methodists. Some of these leaders have swung to the Zinzendorff view, which holds that carnal nature is removed in regeneration. Other leaders, like Rev. J. H. Nichols and Dr. J. B. Barbee, define sanctification in terms of separation from the world and consecration to God. Dr. Barbee has given this definition of sanctification: "Sanctification is a state—a state of being separated from things common and set apart peculiarly and exclusively for a specified object." He also adds: "Sanctification antedates regeneration," and, as "an experience is not possible to any man."

Those in Methodist circles who have looked upon sanctification solely as separation from the world and consecration to God, have confined their emphasis to only one phase of sanctification. They have properly placed large emphasis on separation and consecration, but have overlooked the other side of sanctification, which is that of cleansing on the part of God. We call the attention of the reader again to the prayer of Jesus for his disciples: "Sanctify them through thy truth: thy word is truth." This prayer reveals clearly the important Godward side of sanctification. Separation from the world and consecration is the act of man. The cleansing phase of sanctification is the act of God appropriated by the believer through faith. The prayer of the apostle Paul for believers is like unto that of Jesus, when he prayed: "The God of peace, himself, sanctify you wholly."

The great text on consecration is Romans 12:1, 2. "I beseech you therefore, brethren, by the mercies of God, that ye present your bodies a living sacrifice, holy, acceptable, unto God, which is your reasonable service. And be not conformed to this world: but be ye transformed by the renewing of your mind, that ye may prove what is that good, and acceptable, and perfect will of God." This great text sets forth both separation and cleansing. These elements of holiness are revealed in the words: "Present your bodies" and "Be ye transformed by the renewing of your minds, that ye may prove," or know and do God's "good and acceptable, and perfect will." The consecration is made in order to obtain the much more important work of transformation, renewal, cleansing, and empowering that fit the believer for obedience to God's will

Professor Joseph Agar Beet, D. D., the well known English Wesleyan author and educator, whose books have been used in the courses of study for Methodist preachers, is very clear in his statement relative to sanctification being a definite inward experience, wrought in the heart by God for believers. In his book, "Holiness as Understood by the Writers of the Bible," Dr. Beet says: "The prayers of Christ (John 17:17) and of St. Paul (1 Thess. 5:23) teach plainly that our sanctification is a work of God. And these prayers refer not to the objective holiness

which claims us for God (separation and consecration) but to the subjective holiness (the internal cleansing, love and empowerment) in
which the claimed devotion is actually rendered.
For both prayers were offered on behalf of those
who were already objectively holy (separated
and consecrated).   And the words of Hebrews
12:10, 'that ye may partake of his holiness' implies that our holiness is an outflow of God's holiness, his power working in us the devotion he
requires. . . .   God cannot sanctify the unfor-
given."   Dr. Summers, who has been called "the
greatest theologian of Southern Methodism,"
says: "Sanctification without justification is a
simple absurdity."

CHAPTER XVII

THE HEART CRY FOR THE POWER THAT PREVAILS

The Christian Church has never denied the necessity of holiness, but many and varied views have sprung up in the Church as to when and how we are made holy. The theory that holiness is obtained in regeneration has had a number of strong exponents. In spite of all the efforts to substantiate this view, the predominant testimony of Christian experience stands against it. The Scriptures clearly recognize that regenerated persons described as "in Christ" still possess a carnal nature. A conspicuous example of this type of Christians is spoken of in First Corinthians 3:1-4: "And I brethren could not speak unto you as spiritual, but as unto carnal, even as unto babes in Christ. I have fed you with milk and not with meat; for hitherto ye were not able to bear it, neither yet now are ye able, for ye are yet carnal: for whereas there is among you envy, strife and divisions are ye not carnal and walk as men? For while one saith, I am of Paul; and another, I am of Apollos, are ye not carnal?"

The Protestant Episcopal Church recognizes the validity of this Scripture in their Ninth Article of Religion, which states: "Original sin standeth not in the following of Adam: but is the fault in corruption of every man that nat-

urally is engendered of the offspring of Adam:
and this infection doth remain, yea in those that
are regenerated."

During the writing of these chapters a very
interesting testimony came to me from a distant
state from one who read some of them while
they ran in The Pentecostal Herald. The experience related is characteristic in many phases
of universal Christian experience. A definite
conversion is described briefly: "I grew up under the influence of the Sunday school and
church, and at the age of seventeen had a very
definite experience of conversion at the little
country M. E. Church where we then lived. My
growth in grace was pronounced and rapid..."

A life filled with Christian activity following
this conversion is described as follows: "I have
given myself to the active work of the church
throughout these years, except when deterred
by ill health, and have served in practically
every capacity—Sunday school teacher and superintendent, worker in Epworth League, Missionary activities, evangelistic services, etc. In
the latter God has especially used me in testimony, prayer, personal work, and as a leader of
prayer meetings. As a Sunday school teacher
I have not only been interested in imparting information, but in the winning of souls, and have
used that as I do other forms of Christian activity as an avenue for that purpose.

"My interet in missions has always been

very great, even intense. I have read constantly
for information and try constantly to instill in
others an interest in missions. I hear every
missionary which opportunity affords, and enjoy a wide acquaintance with missionaries on the
field, and have an extensive correspondence with
the same."

The zeal for Bible study and leadership
training following this conversion is also described: "I took many Bible study courses and
leadership training classes for credits in recognized schools, denominational Bible conferences,
etc. In this way I came to know personally many
of our great denominational leaders of whom I
have read so much. I have been a constant and
interested reader of our denominational literature for years. The history, personnel and
standing of our dear Church have always meant
very much to me."

This conversion undoubtedly is characteristic of what we would ordinarily call the highest
and best type of conversion in the church; a conversion bearing fruit in active service in the
church and in equipment for a growing and en-
larged service. And yet in such conversions as
the one we have described, the inner struggle
with a carnal nature that prevented the victory
which the soul longs for, was evident.

The same testimony describes this inward
conflict: "From the time of my conversion I
longed for everything which God had in store

for me, truly hungered after righteousness. Many times upon the call for complete surrender and complete consecration, I have gone forward and knelt at an altar of prayer. At times I thought I had given my all to him, but later learned there were conflicts and doubts and a lack of power and victory in my life. However, after years of praying and trying and longing, 'I let go and let God' and stopped trying and 'began to trust,' and was completely cleansed from unrighteousness and my heart made pure and clean. Truly my life is completely transformed, and since then it has been easy to be a Christian, and easy to do personal work. That was about four years ago. . . . This experience came in a very quiet, unassuming manner, so lacking in anything spectacular that I could hardly believe it all. Oh, the peace and joy and difference since that time! Truly Christ is all in all to me! It is no wonder that I long for the preaching of holiness, and feel it is the greatest need of our churches. I meant to say, that this experience came following a personal interview with Dr. E. Stanley Jones, whom I came to know personally during a week's Bible conference that year."

The preponderence of Christian experience corroborated by a strong array of eminent theologians is to the effect that holiness is not obtained in regeneration but subsequently.

The theory that sanctification is obtained at death has been held by most Calvinists, and in a modified sense by some eminent Methodist theologians. One of the chief among the Methodist theologians holding a modified view of sanctification at death is the Rev. James Mudge, D. D., of the Methodist Episcopal Church. Rev. John R. Brooks, D. D., summarizes the view of Dr. Mudge in his book, "Scriptural Sanctification."

Concerning this view Dr. Brooks says: "That we are in a low sense entirely sanctified in regeneration, but that in the higher sense being saved from all depravity or selfishness, it may not be expected while we are in the body. This is the theory propounded and elaborated with marked ability by the Rev. James Mudge, D. D., of the Methodist Episcopal Church, in his work entitled, 'Growth in Holiness Toward Perfection, or Progressive Sanctification' (1895). Dr. Mudge holds very nearly the views advocated by the authors named above (Zinzendorfinism) as to the thoroughness of the work done in regeneration, differing from them chiefly in setting up an ideal standard of holiness, which he calls 'entire sanctification in a higher or absolute sense,' and which he says cannot be reached until we enter on another life. He teaches 'sanctification up to knowledge' upholds that, as we do not at conversion, and probably never will in this life know all the evil that is in the profound depths of our soul, we may not be thoroughly saved from it before death. And what Mr. Wesley and other Methodist writers call 'sins of infirmity,' resulting from physical depravity, Dr. Mudge seems to regard as the outcroppings of selfishness, or spiritual depravity."

There is, of course, a final salvation which is obtained at death. Primary salvation is obtained in conversion. Full salvation is obtained in sanctification, in the removal of the carnal nature, which may be obtained through faith in the atoning merits of Christ for sanctification, on the part of the believer.

The story has often been told among holiness people about the wife of the Calvinist preacher, who, when facing death, inquired of her husband if she might seek sanctification in view of the approaching death angel. The minister counseled, that it would be well for his wife to seek and obtain this experience in view of the fact that death was at hand. His wife was gloriously sanctified,—but she did not die. The dilemma to the preacher's theology can well be imagined. His wife inquired as to whether or not she should give up her experience, in view of the fact that death had not come. The good judgment of the preacher overbalanced his theological background, and he counseled his wife to keep her experience. But the sequel of this story was more far-reaching than the wife keeping her experience. The husband himself got under conviction from his wife's testimony. The result was that he also sought and obtained the experience of sanctification.

It is blessed indeed that the experience of sanctification is a glorious reality here in this life in spite of all of the theology to the contrary.

CHAPTER XVIII

THE WEIGHT LAID ASIDE

Modern day Methodism has witnessed a number of departures from what is known as the old Wesleyan theory of sanctification as a definite work of grace subsequent to regeneration. One of these departures is the theory that after regeneration we gradually grow into a state of full salvation and perfect love, reached at or before death, but without experiencing any instantaneous or marked change in our experience, and without knowing when such an experience has been attained. Some theologians holding to this view have spoken of entire sanctification as "the zero hour of inbred sin," and yet it is not known when such an hour is reached. The theory is known as *gradual* sanctification, and is sometimes spoken of as "gradualism."

We should keep clearly in mind that the theory of "gradualism" was not the teaching of the early Methodists. Dr. Wilbur F. Tillett, who was for many years Dean of the School of Theology of Vanderbilt University, says: "The real question of issue among Methodists concerning sanctification seems to be this: Does the Bible teach, and Christian experience confirm, the doctrine that there is, subsequent to regeneration, a second radical and instantaneous work of divine grace within and upon the moral nature of the regenerated believer, which must take place before death in order for his complete salvation from all sin?" In speaking of the theory of the early Methodists upon this question, Dr. Tillett says: "That the primitive and generally recognized 'Wesleyan Methodist Doctrine of Sanctification' answers this question affirmatively, admits of easy and abundant truth by an appeal to Wesley, Fletcher, Watson and others."

The notable new departure from this doctrine held by the early Methodists is apparent to every careful observer. Has this departure added to our spiritual power and fervor? Has it helped to spread revivals of religion over the land? In making an observation on this departure from the Wesleyan doctrine of sanctification Dr. Tillett says: "An influential and constantly increasing majority of modern Methodists, however, answer this question negatively . . . . They feel that the doctrine of instantaneous sanctification lacks the Scripture proof which alone can justify its being regarded as a part, least of all an essential part, of the true Bible doctrine of holiness."

Has the negative answer of modern Methodists which Dr. Tillett refers to been prolific in a positive experience? We believe that any candid historian, reviewing the history of primitive Methodists and modern Methodists, will be forced to admit that we have lost, in a very large measure, that positive element in Christian experience which the primitive Methodists enjoyed. Early Methodism was spoken of as "Christianity in earnest." The positive note in the experience of the early Methodists made a profound impression upon the world, and upon other Christian bodies. The spiritual fervor, power and zeal of the early Methodists was spoken of among all denominations, and until this day the leaders of other denominations point to that early period of Methodist history as a typical example of apostolic power and inspiration.

The "gradualism" theory of sanctification has not been prolific in leading Christians into definite victory over the carnal nature. There is, of course, a growth in Christian experience that carries the believer toward this experience as a goal, but there is a definite moment, when, through faith, the believer is cleansed of his carnal nature through the blood of Christ, if he exercises faith for the cleansing. And there is still a growth, and even more rapid, after the carnal nature has been removed. Just as the farmer who dynamites the stumps out of his field will be able to grow more corn and better corn, so the believer will be able to make more rapid progress after the carnal nature has been removed. The perfection of love makes growth toward perfection in character more rapid; so there are always higher heights, deeper depths, and wider horizons for the Christian. The law of growth is not abrogated in the removal of the carnal nature from the believer's heart, but is only augmented.

There are some who hold to the theory of "gradualism" for sanctification who seem to think they are magnifying the law of growth in their theory. And they also seem to think that the theory of instantaneous sanctification subsequent to regeneration is a reproach to the law of growth but such is not the case. Many who hold to this theory have misinterpreted the claims of those who hold to instantaneous sanctification subsequent to regeneration. They have alleged that those who claim to be sanctified have obtained all there is to be obtained; that they have reached the state of finality in salvation. There may be a few misled people who make such a claim, but this is not the teaching of the Wesleyan doctrine of sanctification.

The writer of the epistle to the Hebrews says: "Wherefore seeing we also are compassed about with so great a cloud of witnesses, let us lay aside every weight, and the sin which doth so easily beset us, and let us run with patience the race that is set before us." The apostle here describes an experience that makes for much more rapid progress. His metaphor gives to us the picture of a runner who has suddenly been released from an impediment that enables him to spring forward with a new and increasing stride. This is exactly what happens in the

Christian life when the carnal nature has been removed. The theory of "gradualism" in sanctification claims that "the zero hour of inbred sin" is reached without it being known to the believer. We might raise the question: "Does the runner know it when he has laid aside the weight?" Certainly, the runner knows it, as he leaps forward in a new and increasing stride. So also, and in a much higher and glorious sense, does the Christian know it when the carnal nature has been removed through the cleansing blood of Jesus Christ.

The guilt for the overt acts of sin in regeneration is not removed by growth or by works, but by the cleansing blood of Christ. Regeneration may be preceded by a period of conviction and deep longing for the experience of salvation. We have known many cases where sins were surrendered long in advance in the quest for salvation; but there came a moment and a time when the sinner exercised faith in Christ for his salvation, and in that moment he passed from death unto life, having the guilt of sin removed through the blood of Christ. The same principle holds true relative to the carnal nature as to the guilt of sin. The carnal nature is not removed by growth or by works, but by the cleansing blood of Christ.

It is not necessary for the believer to continue for an indefinite period of time handicapped by "the weight which doth so easily beset us." That sin, which is the weight, may be removed at the moment the believer exercises faith in the cleansing blood of Christ for its removal. The writer to the Hebrews, in his exhortation to the believers to lay aside "the sin which doth so easily beset us" strengthened his exhortation with the testimony of a multitude of witnesses.. He introduces his exhortation with the words: "Wherefore seeing we also are compassed about with so great a cloud of witnesses." Yea, a great cloud of witnesses in heaven and in earth, witness to the fact that "the blood of Jesus Christ his Son cleanseth us from all sin." There is also a great cloud of witnesses, who witness to this cleansing coming as a definite epochal experience subsequent to regeneration, through faith in the cleansing blood of Christ. This uttermost salvation may be obtained by the believer immediately. There is no need of a long, indefinite delay: "Let go, let God," and let the work be done now.

CHAPTER XIX

BARREN CHURCHES

Much is being said today about the need of a revival of religion. The great need is frankly admitted by both the church and the world. A careful review of religious news in the church press for a single week reveals the fact of the great need of a revival in the church.

One religious statistician has made this rather startling statement: "Five per cent of all church members do not exist; ten percent of them cannot be found; twenty-five percent never go to church; fifty percent never contribute a cent to the work of the church; twenty-five percent never attend the mid-week prayer service; ninety percent do not have family worship in their homes; and ninety-five percent never try to win a lost soul to Christ.

The Religious Digest for the month of May, 1937, gives this incident, which reflects something of the impression of the spiritual condition in England and America which has gone abroad. The paragraph describing the incident says: "In despair because his son had become a Christian, a Japanese father sent for the Buddhist priest. To all of the priest's suggestions the father replied sadly that he had found them vain. 'Then, there is only one certain cure,' said the priest finally, 'but it costs a great deal of money.' 'That does not matter,' said the father. 'Well,' replied the priest, 'send him to England or America. There he will be cured.' "

While there is a sense of humor in this incident there is also a tremendous note of tragedy. Conditions have developed in recent years to the state where we have been drifting rapidly toward paganism.

L. A. Reed, writing in The Herald of Holiness, issue of April 24, 1937, says: "It might be interesting to note that there are only two religious groups who are increasing their missionary forces in China, that is the Roman Catholic Church, and the Conservative Fundamentalist Churches. The larger denominations of America, recognized as the Liberal Protestant churches, are withdrawing their missionaries."

The same writer reports a statement of Professor Kenneth Scott Latourette, of Yale University, concerning the present missionary program of the churches. Professor Latourette, who has been a lifelong student of missions, says: "Many, even among the clergy, are seeking in a social revolution a substitute for the religious convictions by which their communions officially stand, but to which they, as individuals, can no longer subscribe. From such a Christianity no vigorous foreign missionary enterprise can be expected. Unless new revivals invigorate it, it is doomed, even in its own stronghold."

The Christian Century (Chicago) is well

known as a modernist religious journal. The editor of this journal observes a vast decay in Christian education. In the issue of the Christian Century, April 28, 1937, the editor says: "Protestantism, the predominant religious group, is near the zero point as a cultural producing influence. Its colleges, founded and long administered as denominational institutions, now conceive themselves as secular institutions, supported by their alumni, and the public of the contiguous regions or cities in which they are located. All allusions as to their possessing any special religious character have vanished. Protestantism has completely surrendered its earlier sense of responsibility to higher education."

A survey by the United Stewardship Council among twenty-one major Protestant denominations, reveals the per capita giving of these churches. The average per capita gift in 1936 for all purposes was $12.28. The average per capita gift of some of the denominations, according to this survey for 1936, was as follows: Church of the Nazarene, $25.55; United Presbyterian, $22.51; Reformed Church in America, $21.71; Moravian, $21.19; Presbyterian (Southern), $19.69; Presbyterian, (Northern) $18.22; Methodist Episcopal, $14.28; Northern Baptist, $13.08; Methodist Episcopal, South, $9.17.

These figures reveal that the Church of the Nazarene is well in the lead of per capita giving among twenty-one of the major denominations in the United States. The per capita giving of the Nazarene Church is almost twice that of the Methodist Episcopal Church, and almost three times that of the Methodist Episcopal Church, South. The Nazarene Church has majored in the preaching of holiness, and it does not seem to have interferred with their giving, or their numerical increase. The fact is they have forged ahead of many of the major denominations in this respect. The teachers and leaders of Methodism who think that the Wesleyan doctrine of sanctification is out of date in this modern age would do well to make a careful survey of the progress of the holiness churches in recent years. It is true that these churches are small numerically in a number of cases, but their comparative progress has been remarkable.

I have previously in these chapters referred to statements of Roger Babson, to the effect that his religious survey reveals that the holiness churches are the only group of churches in the United States which have not shown a decided decline in attendance during recent years.

At a recent session of my own District Conference of the Methodist Episcopal Church, South, the oldest minister in the conference in the point of years of service, stood on the floor and made the statement, that during the past twenty years the Methodist Church had lost ten churches in the district. In the same district the Nazarene Church has gained twelve new churches within four years time.

I am not a Nazarene I am a Methodist. I have been nurtured in the Methodist Church from infancy. My parents dedicated me in holy baptism as an infant at her altar. I was received into her fellowship in early childhood. I received my call to the ministry under her blessed influence. I was educated in her colleges and universities. I was led into the experience of sanctification in one of her colleges. I have served in her ministry in almost every grade of appointment she has to offer, from an eight-point circuit in the Ozark hills of Missouri, to the larger pastorates in the centers of our greatest metropolitan areas. The Methodist Church has been good to me. She has been my spiritual mother, and my life is pledged to her service in the remaining years that may be ahead. But I am greatly concerned about a great spiritual awakening in Methodism. I believe that Methodism could be used to promote a worldwide revival, if she would again place major emphasis upon those distinctive doctrines and standards of living which made her great in the beginning. The distinctive doctrine of primitive Methodism was holiness. The proclamation of this truth was her distinctive message to the world.

The greatest need in our churches today is holiness on the part of the members. Even those theologians who have held that sanctification may come at the time of regeneration, have been frank to admit that in most cases sanctification does not come at the time of regeneration. Rev. T. O. Summers, D. D., recognized as one of the great theologians of Methodism, held that sanctification may be at the time of regeneration. On this point, Dr. Summers says: "If it be possible before regeneration to discover all the depravity of our nature in its diversified features of operations; if we are made thoroughly sensible of its presence, and are as much concerned for its removal as we are for the pardon of our guilt, and the repeal of our condemnation; if, in addition, we have a faith proportionate to such repentance, a faith which is not embarrassed by any doubt, but which covers over the vast extent of the broad commandment and the gracious promise of entire sanctification—we know no reason in the divine economy to prevent the fulfillment of that promise, so that we may be perfectly sanctified in the very moment when we are freely justified."

Dr. Summers also says that most believers are not sanctified at regeneration. On this point he says: "But self knowledge so thorough, and faith so strong and extensive, securing sanctifying grace, so pervading, powerful, perfect, are seldom if ever realized before we are justified and born again. There are few 'babes in Christ' who are not measurably carnal, in consequence of the weakness of their faith, and the defectiveness of their knowledge (1 Cor. 3), few who are not lacking in their faith, while they can say, 'Lord, I believe,'—which is, indeed, a good confession, warranting their claim to a filial relation to God—they have to append the prayer, 'Help thou mine unbelief,' which is an unquestionable acknowledgment of imperfection, even in respect of negative holiness. When there is unbelief or doubt, there must be fear, servile fear, and 'He that feareth is not made perfect in love.' "

The greatest need of the Church today is holiness. Even Dr. Summers, who teaches the possibility of sanctification at the time of regeneration, admits that as a matter of fact very few are sanctified at the time of their regeneration. If this be true, then the great need of the Church on the basis of the reasoning of Dr. Summers, is sanctification. For although he believes that sanctification may be possible in regeneration, very few are actually so sanctified.

Let us again recapture the glorious experience of holiness in the church of Christ and we will again shake the world with a mighty revival of religion.

CHAPTER XX

CRUCIFIED WITH CHRIST

The objections to the experience of holiness as a cleansing from the carnal nature subsequent to regeneration are very similar to objections by unbelievers to the experience of regeneration. A very common objection is that the carnal nature cannot be taken out during this life. In like manner many unbelievers deny the possibility of regeneration. The possibility of the removal of the carnal nature hinges upon the ability of God and the will of God. Is God able to remove the carnal nature? The Scriptures are full of declarations from Genesis to Revelation setting forth God's ability. Paul closes his remarkable prayer, found in the third chapter of Ephesians, with these words: "Now unto him that is able to do exceeding abundantly above all that we ask or think, according to the power that worketh in us, unto him be glory in the church by Christ Jesus throughout all ages, world without end."

In the seventh chapter of Hebrews and the twenty-fifth verse we find another remarkable statement concerning God's ability: "Wherefore he is able to save them to the uttermost that come unto God by him, seeing he ever liveth to make intercession for us." The power of the cleansing blood of Christ is revealed in such scriptural statements as: "The blood of Jesus Christ his Son cleanseth us from all sin." And also: "If we confess our sins, he is faithful and just to forgive us our sins, and cleanse us from all unrighteousness." The statements concerning God's power and ability could be multiplied many fold. There seems to be no shadow of doubt concerning God's ability to remove the carnal nature.

If God is able, we next raise the question: "Is it God's will that the carnal nature be removed?" In the third chapter of the First Epistle of John, and the eighth verse we find these words: "For this purpose the Son of God was manifested, that he might destroy the works of the devil." In the fourth chapter of 1st Thessalonians we find this statement concerning God's will: "For this is the will of God, even your sanctification." Concerning the repetition of Pentecost in the lives of believers for future generations, Peter said: "For the promise is unto you, and unto your children, and unto all that are afar off, even as many as the Lord our God shall call." Jesus prayed for the sanctification of His disciples in His valedictory prayer, which is found in the seventeenth chapter of the Gospel of John: "Sanctify them through thy truth: thy word is truth." Jesus not only prayed for the sanctification of His disciples of that day, but also for the sanctification of His diesciples for all ages to come. His prayer for the sanctification of His disciples in all future ages is expressed in the words: "Neither pray I for these alone, but for them also which shall believe on me through their word." The Scripture seems to leave no doubt but that it is the will of God that the carnal nature be removed. God never intended that the human heart should become a hiding place for the devil. He is able to remove the carnal nature, and He has also willed that it be removed.

Sanctification is the believer's birthright. God has made provision for it in His will, in keeping with His ability to provide an uttermost salvation. It remains, therefore, for the believer to come and obtain his birthright through faith in the cleansing blood of Christ. It would be unreasonable for the heirs of a great estate to live in poverty. It is even more unreasonable for the church to live in spiritual poverty when every provision has been made in the will of God for her to live in triumph and victory. The spiritual leanness in the church today is the occasion of no little comment even on the part of an unbelieving world.

The fires on our altars have burned low. That fervency of spirit which characterized the church of the first century is missing in many of our modern-day churches. I have a Japanese friend who is a remarkable Christian. He is a business man, dealing in Japanese chinaware, and is perhaps the largest salesman of Japanese chinaware in the United States. He was formerly a Buddhist, and very unfriendly to the Christian faith. Some years ago he came under deep conviction through an unusual incident in his life. The awakening which came through this conviction caused him to turn to the church for help. He began attending the leading churches in each city that he visited in his travels as a salesman. In one large city he visited thirty different churches; but in many of these churches he said he met with disappointment. He was a Buddhist seeking salvation, and he wanted to know the way of life. His heart was hungry for God; his soul was carrying a burden of sin. And yet, in church after church which he entered as a hungry soul seeking God, he was given a stone. But eventually he fell into a church where there was spiritual power and fervor, where the message of salvation was sounded from the pulpit, and was witnessed to in the pew. The message found lodgment in the heart of my Japanese friend, and he found Christ as his Savior in a marvelous way. He is today one of the greatest soul winners I know. He has been used as an instrument in leading many of his business friends to Christ. But he still comments on the lack of spiritual power and fervor which he found in the churches, when with a hungry heart he started out to find light concerning the Lord Jesus Christ. There are many such hungry hearts today who are seeking the way of life, and they are disappointed in the spiritual atmosphere which prevails in many churches.

God has willed that His church be a holy church. He has willed that His church march in triumph and victory, overcoming the world. The carnal nature in the hearts of believers is the chief hindrance to a triumphant and victorious church. The removal of the carnal nature through the cleansing blood of Christ brings Pentecost to the modern church just as certainly as Pentecost came to the church of the first century.

But Pentecost means crucifixion. It means the death route. The Apostle Paul said: "I am crucified with Christ." The apostle also said: "Knowing this, that our old man is crucified with him, that the body of sin might be destroyed, that henceforth we should not serve sin."

CHAPTER XXI

SOME OBJECTIONS

One of the common objections to the Wesleyan doctrine of sanctification is that it sets the standards too high, which cannot be obtained in this life. We should bear in mind that the kind of perfection which John Wesley taught was not an absolute perfection which only God has, neither is it an angelic perfection which belongs only to the angels, neither is it an Adamic perfection where the soul is freed from all of those infirmities incident to the fall of man. The kind of perfection which Mr. Wesley taught was a perfection of love. Such a perfection is clearly taught in the Word of God. The Apostle John says: "Perfect love casteth out fear." He also says "He that feareth hath not been made perfect in love." There is a perfection of love which is compatible with infirmities. John Wesley did not regard infirmities as sin, he defined sin as a wilful transgression of a known law of God. His definition is in keeping with the scriptural statement, "Sin is the transgression of the law." We may not expect a perfection in this life which eliminates all infirmities, such as the many mistakes which come from errors in judgment, but we may have a perfection wherein we love God supremely and our fellowman with an abounding love which knows no hate, envy, prejudice or ill will toward any individual.

This perfection of love, as Dr. Curtis has brought to our attention, changes the motive of the Christian from one of duty to one of supreme love. So long as duty is the dominant motive in the Christian life there is something lacking. But when love becomes the supreme motive the Christian enters the high table land of Christian experience. Here new vistas of panoramas unfold with an increasing glory unknown to the Christian where duty was the controlling motive.

Another objection commonly offered to sanctification is the inconsistencies of those who profess the experience. We are ready to grant that these inconsistencies do exist. But if we are to reject sanctification upon this ground, we must also reject regeneration. This is the same objection which the unsaved people in the world often offer for not becoming Christians. They seek to invalidate regeneration on the ground of the inconsistencies of those who have made a profession of the Christian faith. We have met these inconsistencies in both the regenerated and in the sanctified. Jesus met such inconsistencies among His own apostles. The betrayal of Judas does not invalidate the loyalty, faithfulness, and glorious experience of John the beloved. Neither do the inconsistencies of some who profess the experience of sanctification invalidate this glorious experience. Many good examples of this blessed experience may be found all along the pathway of church history even down to our present day.

Another objection offered is "the more holy than thou attitude," which is said to be discovered on the part of those who profess the experience of sanctification. We are frank to admit that some who profess the experience of sanctification do assume such an attitude, but certainly not all who profess the experience assume this attitude. Such an attitude is of course unfortunate. We believe that some people have actually lost the blessedness of this experience through such an unfortunate attitude. While the lives of some may sustain such an objection, there are the lives of others who refute it. One single example in sanctified humility is sufficient to refute this objection. We are confident that these examples are not lacking. I have met a host of such witnesses whose sanctified humility has proven a great benediction to my own life.

Still another objection is that sanctification is lacking in meeting the needs of this modern age in which we live. We are hearing much today about a new age, and a new approach, and even a new theology. Sometime ago I heard a very brilliant professor lecturing in the field of psychology. He referred to the fact that in his youth he had had contact with people who preached and professed the experience of holiness. He had for a time attended a school where the doctrine was given large emphasis. He referred to the inadequacy of the approach of holiness for the present age as compared to the new psychological approach. The trouble with so many new approaches which we hear about today, is, they do not approach. Many of them fail to approach the carnal nature. The approach to the carnal nature with the cleansing blood of Christ is far more important than all of the new approaches that have been presented for this new age in which we live.

The surest way of a proper approach to the social problems of this age is by way of a sanctified church. God demands holiness on the part of His people. When the church pays the price in entire consecration, and exercises faith in the sanctifying merits of the blood of Christ, she has paid the price ot victory that enables her to go forth and grapple with the social problems of the age in a manner otherwise impossible without such an experience.

Another objection raised, is one that claims not to be an objection to the experience, but the witnessing to the experience. Such objectors tell us that it is all right to possess the experience of holiness but that we should not say anything about it. By the same argument Christians should not say anything about regeneration. The objectors say that witnessing to sanctification is a type of boasting which is inconsistent with Christian experience. Of course no testimony should be given, except in a spirit of humility which exalts the Lord Jesus Christ instead of exalting the individual. Some of those who object to witnessing to the experience of sanctification use a statement of Paul found in the third chapter of Philippians, the twelfth verse, to sustain their objection. The words of the passage are, "Not as though I had already attained, either were already perfect: but I follow after, if that I may apprehend that for which also I am apprehended of Christ Jesus." I have really been surprised at the large number of Christians who quote this passage to sustain the objection to witnessing to sanctification. The apostle here is not speaking of Christian perfection in this life but of that perfection which comes in glorification. The verse preceding the one we have quoted gives the explanation which reads: "If by any means I might attain unto the resurrection of the dead." Paul had not yet obtained the perfection of glorification which comes in the life beyond the grave. It was of this perfection he was speaking when he said, "not as though I had already attained, either were already perfect." The apostle immediately follows this statement with a testimony to perfection, found in the fifteenth verse of the same chapter which reads, "Let us therefore, as many as be perfect, be thus minded." The apostle here gives a clear testimony to a type of Christian perfection which is possible in this life. Those who neglect to witness to the experience of sanctification will lose the joy of that experience. The testimony should always be given in humility in such a manner as to exalt Christ rather than the individual.

Another objection has been raised that sanctification divides the church. There are many types of division, some are helpful, some are harmful. The downward division is always harmful. We have had too much of this kind of division in this modern age. It is the downward division of worldliness, indifference and unbelief. The division of modernism denying the fundamentals of the Christian faith has been a downward division, and it has wrought untold harm in the church of God. This division has checked revivals of religion and has brought about a paralysis of spiritual fervor which accounts for much of the spiritual hypocrisy of the present age. The upward division of sanctification is helpful. It is the division of separation from the world. When the experience is properly preached and presented in Christian testimony it is prolific in revivals, in the spread of scriptural holiness, and in lifting the church to higher heights.

There are still others who object to sanctification on the basis that Pentecost is not to be repeated. There is no word of scripture to the effect that Pentecost was for the disciples of the upper room alone. The words spoken by Peter at the conclusion of his sermon on the day of

Pentecost should forever settle the question that Pentecost, as an experience, should be repeated in the church in every age and in the life of every individual. "For the promise is unto you, and to your children, and to all that are afar off, even as many as the Lord our God shall call."

CHAPTER XXII

HOW TO ENTER IN

"What must I do to be sanctified?"

This is a question which comes from earnest, inquiring hearts seeking to enter the Canaan experience of perfect love. This question comes from enlightened believers concerning sanctification just as definitely as a similar question came from the Philippian jailer concerning the way of salvation when he inquired: "Sirs, what must I do to be saved?"

The third and fourth chapters of the Book of Hebrews have very specific teaching concerning a Canaan-rest for Christians which is to be obtained in this life. The entrance of the children of Israel into the Land of Canaan is set forth as a type of the entrance of the believer into a Canaan-rest of Christian experience. In the fourth chapter of Hebrews and the ninth verse we read: "There remaineth therefore a rest to the people of God." There are repeated statements in the third and fourth chapters of Hebrews which indicate that the rest for the people of God spoken of, is to be entered, in this life, through a definite act of faith on the part of the believer. The third verse of the fourth chapter reads in part: "For we which have believed do enter into rest." The first verse of this same chapter reads: "Let us therefore fear, lest, a promise being left us of entering into his rest, any of you should seem to come short of it." The eleventh verse of the same chapter reads: "Let us labor therefore to enter into that rest, lest any man fall after the same example of unbelief." The writer to the Hebrews points out the fact that it was through unbelief that the children of Israel failed to enter the Land of Canaan when they came to Kadesh-Barnea. It was unbelief that turned them back into their wilderness wanderings for a period of forty years. Believers are likewise warned lest they turn back from the sanctified experience through unbelief.

A number of timely warnings and exhortations are given to believers in the third chapter of Hebrews. In verses 7 to 19 of this chapter we read: "Wherefore as the Holy Ghost saith, Today if ye will hear his voice, Harden not your hearts, as in the provocation, in the day of temptation in the wilderness: When your fathers tempted me, proved me, and saw my works forty years. Wherefore I was grieved with that generation, and said, They do always err in their heart; and they have not known my ways. So I sware in my wrath, They shall not enter into my rest. Take heed, brethren, lest there be in any of you an evil heart of unbelief, in departing from the living God. But exhort one another daily, while it is called Today; lest any of you be hardened through the deceitfulness of sin. For we are made partakers of Christ, if we hold

the beginning of our confidence steadfast unto
the end; While it is said, Today if ye will hear
his voice, harden not your hearts, as in the provocation. For some, when they had heard, did
provoke: howbeit not all that came out of Egypt
by Moses. But with who, was he grieved forty
years? was it not with them that had sinned,
whose carcasses fell in the wilderness? And to
whom sware he that they should not enter into
his rest, but to them that believed not? So we
see that they could not enter in because of unbelief."

Before the children of Israel could enter Canaan it was necessary for them to cross the Red
Sea. The first necessary step was to get out of
Egypt. The deliverance from Egypt is a type
of deliverance from the bondage of sin. Before
the soul can enter the Canaan experience of perfect love there must first be deliverance from the
Egyptian bondage of sinful transgression. The
sinful soul needs pardon and forgiveness before
becoming a candidate for sanctification. The removal of the guilt of sin which comes through
overt acts is needed before the soul becomes a fit
candidate for cleansing from the being of sin.
We must be regenerated whereby we become
new creatures before we are fit candidates for
sanctification whereby we become wholly consecrated creatures with "bodies a living sacrifice,
holy, acceptable unto God."

Dr. H. C. Morrison, in an editorial in The

Pentecostal Herald, bearing date of September the 15th, 1937, quotes some very striking statements from John Wesley on this subject, which statements we give in the following paragraphs.

John Wesley recognized regeneration as a requisite step preceding sanctification. Six years before his death Mr. Wesley wrote the Rev. Freeborn Garretson, saying: "It will be well, as soon as any of them find peace with God, to exhort them to go on to perfection. The more explicitly and strongly you press all believers to aspire after entire sanctification as obtainable now by simple faith, the more the whole work of God will prosper."

During this same year, 1785, Mr. Wesley wrote Rev. John Oglive: "God will prosper you in your labors, especially if you constantly and strongly exhort all believers to expect full sanctification now by simple faith."

The evidence seems conclusive that John Wesley never changed his view of sanctification as a definite work of grace subsequent to regeneration as some modern leaders have endeavored to set forth in their efforts to discredit the doctrine so universally held by early Methodists.

Under date of September the 15th, 1790, only five months and seventeen days before his death, (see Wesley, Vol. 7, P. 153), Mr. Wesley wrote Robert Carr Brackenburg, Esq.: "I am glad Brother D. has more light with regard to

full sanctification. This doctrine is the grand
deposit which God has lodged with the people
called Methodists; and for the sake of propa-
gating this chiefly he appears to have raised us
up."

Under date of Nevember the 26th, 1790, only
three months and six days before his death, Mr.
Wesley wrote to Adam Clarke: "If we can prove
that any of our leaders, either directly or indi-
rectly, speak against it, (perfect love), let him
be a preacher or a leader no longer. I doubt
whether he should continue in the Society, because he that could speak thus in our congregations cannot be an honest man."

Only thirty-one days before his death Mr.
Wesley wrote to Rev. John Booth: "Whenever
you have the opportunity of speaking to believers, urge them to go on to perfection. Spare no
pains, and God, even our God, will give you His
blessing." Only four days before his death,
which occurred March the 2nd, 1791, on Febru-
ary the 27th, Mr. Wesley said: "We must be
justified by faith, and then go on to full sanctification."

The first step toward sanctification is, "Be
sure of your salvation." In my experience of
more than twenty years as a pastor I have found
that the best people in my church are the first to
become seekers after sanctification when the
truth is presented in a Scriptural manner. The
backslider is not a fit candidate for sanctifica-

tion because he needs first, reclamation. The sinner is not a fit candidate because he needs first, salvation.

The sinner cannot be forgiven until he surrenders every sin, and exercises faith in Christ as his personal Savior. The Christian cannot be sanctified until he consecrates every gift and every talent, and exercises faith in the altar to sanctify the gift. There is an altar for the consecration of the Christian. This altar is spoken of in the 13th chapter of Hebrews, and the 10th verse: "We have an altar, whereof they have no right to eat which serve the tabernacle. For the bodies of those beasts, whose blood is brought into the sanctuary by the high priest for sin, are burned without the camp, Wherefore Jesus also, that he might sanctify the people with his own blood, suffered without the gate." The reference in this passage is to the sin offering, which the priests were not allowed to eat. The law required them to carry it out beyond the lines of the encampment, and utterly consume it with fire. In this we have a type of how God deals with sin, extermination.

The sin offering is a type of the human life of Christ which was completely exterminated outside of the walls of Jerusalem for the sins of the whole world. Christ's atoning death upon the cross included both redemption for a guilty world, and sanctification for a redeemed church. The altar which the Christian has for his consecration as spoken of in the 10th verse of the 13th chapter of Hebrews, is the cross of Calvary, on which the Lamb of God bled and died.   It is the merit of Christ's atoning death for the sanctification of the church.

A very definite exhortation is made to the Christian in the New Testament, to consecrate his all upon this altar.   In the 12th chapter of Romans, and the 1st verse, the Apostle Paul gives this exhortation: "I beseech you. therefore, brethren, by the mercies of God, that ye present your bodies, a living sacrifice, holy, acceptable unto God, which is your reasonable service." When the Christian consecrates all, he may then claim and appropriate for himself the promise which says: "Jesus also, that he might sanctify the people with His own blood, suffered without the gate;" and also the promise which says: "Christ also loved the church, and gave himself for it; that he might sanctify and cleanse it with the washing of water by the word, that he might present it to himself a glorious church, not having spot, or wrinkle, or any such thing; but that it should be holy and without blemish."   When the complete consecration is made and these promises are appropriated by faith, the work is done.   Jesus then becomes to the soul not only Savior, but Lord.   He not only saves, but He sanctifies.

With this faith the Christian knows the reality of Paul's statement: "Knowing this, that our Old Man is crucified with him, that the body of sin might be destroyed, and that henceforth we should not serve sin." The Christian who has had the strife of two natures within until he has cried, "O wretched man that I am; who shall deliver me from the body of this death?" is able now to exclaim in triumph: "I thank God through Jesus Christ our Lord!"

CHAPTER XXIII

A GREAT MISSIONARY ENTERS IN

The story of Hudson Taylor and the China Inland Mission comprises one of the thrilling romances in modern missionary endeavor. Much has been said and written in recent years about the retrenchment of some of the missionary boards of the large and well established denominations. These retrenchments have given cause for grave concern on the part of the leaders of these churches. In more than one instance the number of missionaries has been cut by one-half by some of the great denominational Boards. Giving to the cause of missions has declined to an alarming degree with a number of the denominations. This decline has been attributed for the most part to the years of depression. There is, however, another angle to this whole situation which is of tremendous interest. It is the fact that during this period of depression and retrenchment on the part of many of the great missionary boards of the country, a number of missionary societies, mostly the faith missions, did not suffer any decrease or curtailment in their missionary program during the period when the great missionary boards found it necessary to cut their programs in two by one-half.

Dr. Robert Hall Glover, Home Director of

the China Inland Missions in an address
before the Reformed Presbyterian Church Mission Board on the decline in missionary giving
in recent years, said: "But that the depression is
not the sole cause of this falling off in the missionary gifts can easily be established by reference to the records of various boards, which
show that the decline in amounts donated to missions began some time before the depression set
in, when this country was enjoying a wave of
material prosperity. While it would be foolish
to deny that the depression has played some part
in reduced missionary revenue it must be admitted that this was not the sole cause of such
reduction, nor yet the initial cause. For myself
let me express the firm conviction that it was not
really the main cause. In the support of this assertion I need only cite the fact that certain societies, the China Inland Mission among them,
had not suffered a decrease in donations, nor any
curtailment of their field operations, but on the
contrary had throughout the depression gone
steadily on, and added to their staff of workers,
and have made substantial advances in the
field." A footnote to the address of Dr. Glover,
which was printed in the June, 1937, issue of
Revelation, makes this statement concerning
gifts to the China Inland Mission during the depression years. "Donations to the China Inland
Mission during the seven year period from the
beginning of the depression have amounted to

considerably more than in the preceding seven-year period. During the past seven years (1930 to 1936 inclusive), 629 new missionaries were sent out, and more than 100 new main stations were opened on the field."

The great empire of China is one of the most alluring countries upon the face of the earth. The story of Hudson Taylor and the China Inland Mission has to do with the great interior of China, with a population of more than two hundred millions of souls. Hudson Taylor had the vision of a faith mission in the heart of China in the period between 1860 and 1865. He launched it upon the principle of exercising absolute faith and trust in God for all of the needs of the mission. Hudson Taylor's missionary party of eighteen souls sailed from London on the 26th day of May, 1866. After months of travel, and passing through a storm of fifteen days duration, which all but wrecked the ship, they landed in Shanghai on a beautiful September Sunday of that same year. Another long and perilous journey was ahead of them in order to reach the far interior of China, where they were to carry on their work. The many providences of God which watched over them on the journey to the interior and in getting established in their work is a thrilling chapter of miraculous guidance, divine protection, and answer to prayer. You cannot read this story without recognizing the reality of God, and His presence in the every day lives of those who dare to trust Him.

The work grew from the very beginning, and the results in many cases went far beyond their expectations. But certainly it was not an easy task. The hardships which they endured can hardly be properly appraised by those of us who live in a land like the United States, where we enjoy so many comforts and blessings of life.

In the living quarters, which they found in most of the places, there were many hardships to encounter. There was a prevalence of cockroaches and rats at night which were a menace while they endeavored to sleep. So it was not uncommon for many of their nights to be disturbed by these unfriendly pests. The missionaries went upon the principle that they were willing to endure any hardship that they might carry the gospel to the millions of people who had never heard the wonderful story. With a faithfulness and perseverance that causes us to marvel, they pursued their work in the face of every obstacle and opposition without complaint.

Within a few years after their arrival in the city of Yang-Chow the missionaries were the victims of a riot, in which a number of them were severely beaten and wounded, and they barely escaped with their lives. The casualties of that riot is described by one of the missionaries: "Mr. Reed lay groaning with pain, the poor, tired children wanted to sleep, but we dared not let them, as at any moment we might have to flee again. Mrs. Taylor was almost fainting from loss of blood; and I now found that my arm was bleeding from a bad cut, and so painful that I could not move it, while most of us were stiff and sore with bruises."

In writing to the headquarters of the mission in London, Mr. Taylor spoke of the requirements of a missionary, and of the sacrifices which they would be expected to undergo when coming to China. He said: "China is not to be won for Christ by self-seeking, ease-loving men and women. Those not prepared for labor, self-denial, and many discouragements will be poor helpers in the work. In short, the men and women we need are those who will put Jesus, China, and souls foremost in everything and at all times: life itself must be secondary. . . . Of such men, of such women, do not fear to send us too many. Their price is far above rubies."

In the year 1869, three years after the missionaries had begun their great work in the interior of China, a great epoch in spiritual experience came to Hudson Taylor and a number of his missionaries. If any group on earth had entered the fulness of the sanctified life it would seem that this group had. They were living by faith in a missionary field that others had refused to enter. They had had many conversions, and were witnessing remarkable answers to

prayer day by day. But the missionaries themselves, including Hudson Taylor, their leader,
faced an internal strife in their own personal
Christian experiences. It was about this time
that a series of articles was published in a religious journal known as The Revival,—later
named The Christian,—on the subject: "The
Way of Holiness." These articles fell into the
hands of the missionaries, and they read them
with much interest. A statement in one of the
articles said: "Surely the words 'For me to live
is Christ.' cannot mean less than habitual victory over sin." A testimony in one of these articles said: " 'Purifying their hearts by faith':
how my soul leaps up at those words, seeing in a
moment the possibility of deliverance! "If
then it is by faith,' I exclaim, 'I will trust Jesus
for a pure heart, and now!' "

It was Mr. McCarthy, a member of the missionary band, who first came to the place in
Christian experience where he could give the
above testimony. Soon after this he met Hudson
Taylor, his leader, and said: "I do wish I could
have a talk with you now about the way of holiness." And Mr. McCarthy did talk to Hudson
Taylor about this way. A little later, while ab-
sent from Mr. MaCarthy in another city, Hudson Taylor was reading a letter he had received
from him upon this same subject. The light
broke upon his soul, which he describes in these
words: "As I read I saw it all. I looked to Je-

sus; and when I saw, Oh, how joy flowed!" Soon
after this, when Hudson Taylor was calling on
one of his patients, Mr. Judd, the patient described the meeting as follows: "When I went
to welcome him he was so full of joy that he
scarcely knew how to speak to me. He did not
even say, 'How do you do?' Walking up and
down the room with his hands behind him he ex-
claimed: 'Oh, Mr. Judd, God has made me a new
man! God has made me a new man!'" Later,
Mr. Judd gave the following description of what
had happened to the great missionary leader,
who had forsaken home, friends, and had risked
his all for the evangelization of Inland China.
"He was a joyous man now," added Mr. Judd, "a
bright, happy Christian. He had been a toiling,
burdened one before, with latterly not much rest
of soul. It was resting in Jesus now, and letting
Him do the work—which makes all the difference! Whenever he spoke in meetings after
that, a new power seemed to flow from him, and
in the practical things of life a new peace possessed him. Troubles did not worry him as before. He cast everything on God in a new way,
and gave more time to prayer. Instead of working late at night, he began to go to bed earlier,
rising at five in the morning to give two hours
before the work of the day began to Bible study
and prayer. Thus his own soul was fed, and
from him flowed the living water to others."

CHAPTER XXIV.

THE VICTORY OF PERPETUAL CONQUEST

The Apostle Paul encountered a storm on the Mediterranean Sea, but he lifted that storm out of the ordinary, and immortalized it upon the pages of history, because he touched it with his prayers, his faith, and his love for the souls of men.

The significance of that storm which crossed the pathway of the Apostle Paul must be weighed in the light of some previous events in his life. We go back for a few years in the life of the apostle to a turbulent day in the city of Jerusalem.

Paul went to Jerusalem against the advice of his friends, and some of the prophets of his day. They warned him that if he went he would be bound. His reply was, "I am ready not to be bound only, but also to die at Jerusalem for the name of the Lord Jesus." On that day Paul had been summoned before the Sanhedrin to answer to certain accusations of the Jews. When he told the Sanhedrin that he had lived in all good conscience before God, Annas, the high priest, commanded them that stood by to smite him on the mouth. In the course of the discussion before the Sanhedrin, Paul reminded them of the fact that he was a Pharisee. This threw the Sanhedrin into confusion, arraying the Pharisees and the Sadducees against each other.   The dissension which arose was so great that Claudius Lysias the chief captain, fearing that Paul would be pulled in pieces, commanded the soldiers to take him by force from amongst them and bring him into the castle.

On the night following that turbulent day we read: "The Lord stood by him and said, Be of good cheer, Paul: for as thou hast testified of me at Jerusalem, so must thou bear witness also at Rome."   The Apostle Paul was given the assurance that he was to see Rome.   This was indeed a blessed message.   It was a glorious assurance.   It was a comfort to his soul in the midst of the great opposition which raged against him.   But this comfort and this assurance did not waiver trials and testings along the way, including the terrible storm at sea.   The assurance of answered prayer does not mean the waiver of testings, severe obstacles, or even a storm at sea before the prayer comes to fruition. But the Lord stood before Paul in the castle at the close of that day, and told him that he would see Rome.   He did not mean that the road would be easy, and that the sailing would be smooth, on his journey to the "Eternal City."

The crossing of the Jordan by the Israelites into the land of Canaan was a great advance through faith.   It was a great epochal experience in the history of Israel, typifying an entire consecration on the part of the Christian, culmi-

nating in sanctification. As you recall, the
Children of Israel came to a testing at Kadesh-
Barnea, and failed to enter the Land of Promise, due to their unbelief. After turning back
into the wilderness for a period of wandering
for forty years, they came to Canaan. Canaan
was their goal in these years of wanderings. So
it was a day of great triumph after the turning
back at Kadesh-Barnea, and after forty years of
wilderness life, to enter the Promised Land. The
entry into the Promised Land was accompanied
by much shouting. Their first great victory was
the capture of the City of Jericho, whose walls
fell amid the blowing of their trumpets, and the
triumphs of their shouts of victory. But this
glorious entrance and this mighty triumph did
not mean that the days of testing and of conquest were over. A land to be conquered stretch-
ed out before them. There were many battles
ahead to be fought. There were many victories
to be won if they were true to God. God told
them as they entered the land that the victories
which they failed to win would become as pricks
in their eyes, and thorns in their sides. This
warning of the Lord is found in the 33rd chapter
of Numbers, and the 55th verse: "But if ye will
not drive out the inhabitants of the land from
before you; then shall come to pass, that those
which ye let remain of them, shall be pricks in
your eyes, and thorns in your sides, and shall
vex you in the land wherein ye dwell."

We should ever bear in mind that in connection with every assurance of God concerning answered prayer, in connection with every command of God to go forward, and in connection with the great experiences of the Christian life in regeneration, the witness of the Spirit, and sanctification, there are always battles to be fought, testings to be met, and storms at sea to be encountered. These testings and the storms at sea make possible perpetual conquest. Paul was privileged not only to receive the blessed assurance from the Lord while in the prison at Jerusalem, that he would see Rome, but he was likewise privileged to obtain the many blessings which came from the testings on the journey to Rome, including the encounter with the storm at sea. The Children of Isreal were privileged not only to raise a shout of victory when they crossed into the Promised Land, but also to raise a shout of many victories coming through the contests and the encounters in that land as they went forth to subdue it in the name of the Lord.

Paul encountered the storm at sea through no fault of his own. In the course of the journey they came to a place which was called The Fair Havens on the Island of Crete. Paul counseled against the ship putting out to sea from this place. He said to the officers of the ship: "Sirs, I perceive that this voyage will be with hurt and much damage, not only of the lading and ship, but also of our lives." But his counsel went unheeded, as indicated in these words of the Scripture: "Nevertheless the Centurion believed the master and the owner of the ship, more than those things which were spoken by Paul. And because the haven was not commodious to winter in, the more part advised to depart thence also, if by any means they might attain to Phenice, and there to winter; which is an haven of Crete, and lieth toward the southwest and northwest. And when the south wind blew softly, supposing that they had attained their purpose, loosing thence they sailed close by Crete." The fair sailing was soon followed by a storm, as is expressed in the words: "But not long after there arose against it a tempestuous wind, called Euroclydon."

This passage of Scripture concerning Paul's counsel to the ship's crew at The Fair Havens throws a flood of light upon his character. We are profoundly impressed with the apostle's prayer life. We should bear in mind that he did not wait until he encountered a storm to pray. Paul was engaged in prayer at The Fair Havens when the sky was clear, when the sea was calm, and no storm was in sight. How did it happen that Paul, who had never traveled over this course of the sea before was a better weather prophet than the veteran seamen? The answer is to be found in his prayer life. He talked intimately with his Lord in prayer. His prayer life at The Fair Havens was just as consistent as in the day of a storm. Through prayer he had obtained a direct revelation concerning the storm that was ahead. If we keep up the prayer life at The Fair Havens, our prayers will be effective when the storm breaks. Some people become very penitent and prayerful in the day of storm, but they lack the background of prayer life at The Fair Havens. If we pray as we should when the sky is clear, our prayers will penetrate the clouds when they hide the face of the sun. Too much emphasis cannot be placed upon the importance of prayer in the every day life, and also of the importance of praying about the ordinary things of life. Paul prayed daily about his journey when he traveled. He committed the outcome of his journey to God rather than to the captain of the ship.

The revelations which came to Paul through answered prayer, and the triumph of his faith, did not pre-empt him from suffering from the blunders and the mistakes of other people. If the captain of the crew had listened to the counsel of Paul, the storm would have been avoided; but the captain listened to man rather than the revelation of God which came through the Apostle Paul. As Christians we will be called upon to endure many a testing, and reap many a painful harvest coming through the mistakes and blunders of other people. Our faith is even more sorely tried when we are called upon to face the testings which come through the mistakes of others, than when the testings come through our own mistakes. The storm was even a greater test to the Apostle Paul, when he realized that it could have been avoided, had the captain listened to his counsel. This fact is reflected in the words of Paul: "Sirs, ye should have hearkened unto me, and not have loosed from Crete, and to have gained this harm and loss." We will complain much quicker when the mistakes of another pinch us, than when our own mistakes pinch us. One of the conquests which we are called upon to make in the Christian life, is to encounter with triumph, the storms which cross our pathway unnecessarily, save for the mistakes and blunders of other people. So Paul was called upon, not only to pass through the storm, but also to obtain victory over the fact, that he encountered the storm due to men going contrary to the advice which had come to him as a revelation through prayer.

The consistency of the prayer life of Paul in the day of sunshine made his praying normal and natural in the day of the storm. Many people pray when the storm breaks, who have neglected prayer in the day of sunshine. They come to God for help, but they come weakened through neglect of prayer and Bible study. In the day of sunshine they neglected prayer and Bible study, therefore in the day of the storm their prayers failed to penetrate the clouds. Blessed is the man who is in intimate fellowship with the

Heavenly Father, in the day when the storm breaks.

Paul prayed and fasted until the angel of the Lord stood by, and gave him the blessed assurance that their lives would be saved, although the ship would be wrecked. At the end of fourteen days Paul gave the captain and the crew the assurance of his answered prayer. His message to that panic-stricken crew, after having been tempest tossed for fourteen days, was: "I exhort you to be of good cheer; there shall be no loss of any man's life among you, but of the ship. For there stood by me this night the angel of God, whose I am, and whom I serve, saying, Fear not, Paul, thou must be brought before Cæsar: lo, God hath given thee all of them that sail with thee. Therefore, sirs, be of good cheer: for I believe God, that it shall be even as it was told me." Paul, the man of prayer, becomes the captain of the ship. His message in the midst of the storm was, "Be of good cheer." Paul's testimony in the midst of the storm was a fulfillment of the Scripture which says: "This is the victory that overcometh the world, even your faith." It was even so as Paul predicted. At last he entered Rome, according to the statement of the Lord, who appeared to him in the prison at Jerusalem when He said: "Be of good cheer, Paul: for as thou hast testified of me in Jerusalem, so must thou bear witness also at Rome."

Paul not only came to Rome, according to the

word of the Lord, after encountering the dangers of many snares and pitfalls, and the terrible storm, but also he finally came to heaven, with a triumphant faith and a blessed assurance which he expressed in the immortal words: "For I am now ready to be offered, and the time of my departure is at hand. I have fought a good fight, I have finished my course, I have kept the faith: henceforth there is laid up for me a crown of righteousness which the Lord, the righteous judge, shall give to me at that day: and not to me only, but unto all of them also that love his appearing."

The Power That Prevails enables us to triumph in The Victory of Perpetual Conquest, so that we, "beholding as in a mirror the glory of the Lord, are transformed in the same image from glory to glory." This increasing glory which comes through the victories of perpetual conquest enables us to ascend toward the topless heights with horizons that are ever widening in time and in eternity. "Thanks be to God, which giveth us the victory through our Lord Jesus Christ."

THE END

www.ingramcontent.com/pod-product-compliance
Lightning Source LLC
Chambersburg PA
CBHW021153020426
42331CB00003B/31